WHEN MAN BECOMES PREY

Fatal Encounters with North America's Most Feared Predators

CAT URBIGKIT

LYONS PRESS
Guilford, Connecticut
Helena, Montana
An imprint of Rowman & Littlefield

The photographs in this book are of a combination of wild and captive animals. At least one of the grizzly bears photographed for the book was present at the scene of two human fatalities.

Lyons Press is an imprint of Rowman & Littlefield.

Distributed by NATIONAL BOOK NETWORK

Copyright © 2014 by Cat Urbigkit

Map by Melissa Baker © Rowman & Littlefield
All photos by the author.
Food hanging illustrations on page 30 © Rowman & Littlefield

British Library Cataloguing-in-Publication Information available

Library of Congress Cataloging-in-Publication Data

Urbigkit, Cat.
  When man becomes prey : fatal encounters with North America's most feared predators /
Cat Urbigkit.
     pages cm
  Includes bibliographical references and index.
  ISBN 978-0-7627-9129-3
  1. Animal attacks—North America. 2. Carnivora—Behavior—North America. I. Title.
  QL100.5.U73 2014
  591.5'3—dc23
                       2014019173

CONTENTS

INTRODUCTION

Grizzly and black bears, mountain lions, coyotes, and wolves all roam diverse landscapes of North America, expanding their ranges from remote wildlands to suburbia. Although these North American predators were once hunted, trapped, poisoned, shot, and otherwise persecuted nearly to the point of extinction, those days are long past. Changing public attitudes toward predators have resulted in a more conservation-oriented approach to predator management in the last few decades, and many predator populations are now thriving, expanding in both numbers and distribution. At the same time, more people in North America are living in areas with large carnivore and other predator populations than at any time in history. The expansion of predator populations, paired with the rise in the human population across the same range, is a formula for increased conflicts between man and beast.

This book examines and attempts to classify real-life encounters between humans and five North American predator species that have inflicted fatal injuries on humans: black bears, grizzly bears, mountain lions, coyotes, and gray wolves. Some of these species are so abundant they have become common, and some regions of North American are home to all five species across the same range, as demonstrated on the maps on pages x–xi.

It is important to understand the circumstances in which human encounters with predators result in human injury or death, so that recommendations can be made to reduce the likelihood of further fatal attacks. Rather than providing a comprehensive list of all attacks by a particular predator, this book outlines some of the observed predator and human behaviors that resulted in human injury, as well as recounts some of the most recent attacks. In many cases, certain factors and predator behaviors can be identified that indicate an increased risk of attack. The common thread of these predator attacks on humans is that the animals no longer exhibited a fear of humans.

Those who discount the threat posed by wild predators often note that a person has a greater chance of being struck by lightning than of being attacked by a predator. What that fails to acknowledge is that the risk of being attacked by a wild predator is higher when humans are within territories inhabited by wild predators. Mail carriers, for example, have a higher risk of dog bites than other members of the population, and that is because mail carriers enter into dog territories to deliver mail to their human owners. The simple fact is that increases in both human and predator populations come with an increased risk of predator attacks on humans.

Some point the finger of blame on humans as the cause of human/wildlife conflicts, because humans may live or recreate in predator habitat. But there is little point in casting blame. In reality, predators have moved into habitats that were constructed or enriched by humans. For example, many urban housing projects include provisions for open parks, greenbelts, and other natural features that improve existing landscapes in a way that allows prey populations to thrive at higher densities than in the past, with predator populations

soon expanding into these areas, and, in some cases, at much higher levels than in neighboring regions. Irrigated landscaping and installation of lush vegetative components provide cover and food for prey species such as rabbits, rodents, and even larger game species, such as deer. It's a logical sequence that predators (such as coyotes and mountain lions) soon follow.

In his 2012 book, *Nature Wars: The Incredible Story of How Wildlife Comebacks Turned Backyards into Battlegrounds*, Jim Sterba discusses the problems caused by overabundant white-tailed deer populations and notes that, as residential sprawl spread throughout the eastern United States, much of the land was closed to hunting—either through landowners posting No Hunting signs or through the enactment of laws prohibiting the discharge of firearms in not just small areas but entire townships and counties. The result has been that "hundreds of thousands of square miles in the heart of the white-tailed deer's historic range were largely off-limits to one of its biggest predators"—humans. With people unable to control the deer populations, predators moved into areas with this rich prey base, and conflicts were inevitable under such circumstances. Finding a mountain lion on your lawn feeding on a freshly killed deer is certainly unnerving, but considering the alternatives, it's better the deer than you.

The attitude of "it's our fault because they were here first" holds little merit in discussions of human conflicts with predators. Since human development results in land improvements that prey species find attractive, predators make more use of these areas. It is the very nature of wild predators to take advantage of available resources.

Research on the use of residential areas by mountain lions in western Washington found that 93 percent of collared lions used residential areas. This use appeared to be a function of the adaptive and mobile nature of the mountain lion—a species keenly suited to exploiting suitable habitat and resources within residential areas.

When predators enter areas of human development and are involved in conflict, there is usually someone offering up the explanation that the animals only did so because they were starving, or experiencing some shortage of natural foods. However, this is rarely the case.

For example, a 2013 paper on foraging behavior of black bears near human developments in and around Missoula, Montana, noted: "Black bears foraged on human foods near houses even when wildland foods were available, suggesting that the absence of wildland foods may not influence the probability of bears foraging near houses. Additionally, other attractants, in this case fruit trees, appear to be more important than the availability of garbage in influencing when bears forage near houses."

We humans like to have resource-rich environments, but need to be more thoughtful about how we go about sharing that environment with our wild neighbors.

Changing social attitudes toward predators also appears to have an influence on the frequency of predator attacks on humans. Increased tolerance for wild animals near humans can cause a chain reaction in which the animals lose their fear of humans, eventually

leading to attacks on their human neighbors. The areas where the most severe predator attacks on humans examined in this book occur are within or near places where hunting or other persecution of predators is not allowed—within municipal areas, state parks, and national parks.

Many predator attacks on humans are not random, unpredictable events. There is often a pattern of observed circumstances and animal behaviors that indicate an attack on a human may be imminent. Although some attacks are the result of surprise encounters, some predators regard humans as prey. Through recounting real-life animal encounters and analyzing these stories, this book will help you learn about the differences in predator attacks and provide guidance on how to avoid or minimize such encounters. This book does not include encounters involving rabid animals.

We have made great progress in providing for recovery and conservation of a variety of wild predators, but it is important that we know all we can about the circumstances of serious attacks on humans. The future of our human relationship with predators is reliant on this knowledge. Norwegian researchers Jonny Löe and Eivin Röskaft reviewed large carnivore attacks and human safety for the Royal Swedish Academy of Sciences and noted that attacks by large carnivores that result in human injury or death "may undermine conservation efforts by resulting in negative attitudes toward such efforts and more illegal hunting." Most importantly, the researchers noted, "A large carnivore that has attacked a human being in a predatory manner may attack again."

Human behavior during an attack can influence the outcome of the attack, and even prevent attacks. Researchers have found certain patterns of attack, and we can benefit from those findings, following behavioral recommendations that can help reduce our risk of attack, or minimize the severity of injury during such an attack.

Large predators have always posed a threat to humans, and likely always will. The purpose of this book is not to generate a high level of fear but instead to relay factual information with the hope of increasing public understanding of predators and predator behavior.

Wild predators are not lovable toys to be enjoyed when convenient and then discarded or destroyed when they reveal their true nature. Predators should be treated with a realistic acknowledgment that they are animals that kill prey to survive, and should be respected for the wild creatures they are.

RANGE OF SPECIES

Black Bear

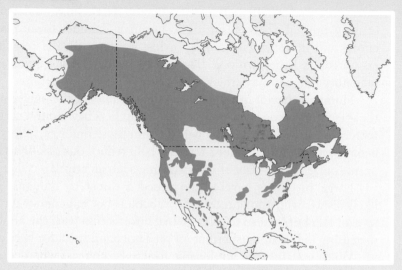

Coyote

Gray Wolf

Mountain Lion

Grizzly Bear

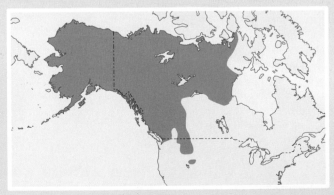

Chapter 1

Black Bears

Jake Francom awoke in his tent in a Utah campground at 5:30 a.m. on June 17, 2007, to the sensation of claws grasping at his skull. A black bear was attacking him through the side of the tent, hitting Francom several times as it clawed its way inside the tent. When Francom tried to sit up, the bear pushed him back down, with one paw slashing the tent open and ripping his pillow. Francom yelled to his buddies in nearby tents for help as he struggled to escape his tent and the grasping claws.

Firing their guns into the air and yelling, the men scared the bear away from their camp. But when the bear was 50 yards away, it sat down on its haunches and looked back at the group of people. The men once again took up their pursuit of the bold bruin, throwing rocks and yelling at the bear to fully scare him away.

Now that they were up, Francom and his friends looked around and saw the bear had ransacked their campsite, raiding and damaging the coolers sitting outside their tents. They were camped in a dispersed campsite in Utah's American Fork Canyon in the Uinta National Forest. This was a popular camping spot, although it had no water or bathroom facilities. The fire pit, log bench, flat spot for tents, and parking spot off the roadway made it a cozy campsite for recreationalists in this scenic national forest. The US Forest Service managed the campground, and charged a fee of $13 per night for use of the site, which was accessed by a forest service road.

Francom called in the bear attack to the Utah County Sheriff's Office Dispatch. The dispatcher said she would notify the forest service about the incident, while Francom should contact state wildlife officials.

This is when the system failed.

Although a forest service law enforcement officer was notified about the incident, and despite promises otherwise, that officer did not contact anyone else in her agency, or take any action of any kind in response to the bear attack. No one else in the forest service knew about the incident, and no action was taken to warn other campers about the potential danger.

Francom was able to notify state wildlife officials, and they did take action. The Utah Division of Wildlife Resources has a three-level classification system for problem bears. The highest classification is Level III, for bears that have shown no fear of humans, have displayed aggressive behavior toward humans, and are deemed a threat to public safety. Utah officials immediately classified the bear as a Level III nuisance—the high-danger classification that acknowledges the animal must be destroyed. Two wildlife officials with tracking dogs were brought in to track the bear, but were unsuccessful despite five hours of effort. The team concluded its search around 5 p.m. the same day of the attack, deciding to attempt to trap the bear the next morning from the Francom campsite, which was empty since Francom and his friends had departed the scene. One of the two state bear trackers later acknowledged that the Francom campsite was the best place to attempt to trap the bear, since it would likely return to that location.

Sam Ives's family didn't know any of this when they arrived at the campsite that evening. They had no idea that a bear had attacked a man in his tent at the same campsite just twelve hours before. They checked in with the forest service campground host before proceeding to the campsite. The campground host had not been told of the earlier bear attack, so he could not and did not relay any information to the family seeking out a camping spot for the night. The family set up camp, cooked dinner, cleaned up, packed their gear away, and climbed into their multichambered tent to sleep. It was a great end to Father's Day. Eleven-year-old Sam crawled into the smaller compartment of the two-room tent. Without his parents knowing it, Sam snacked on a granola bar and placed the empty wrapper in a pocket of the tent.

Sometime during the night, the black bear that had attacked Jake Francom just hours before returned to the campsite where the family slept. It ripped open the side of the tent where Sam slept, grabbing the boy and killing him. His parents heard a noise and got up to have a look around, but were unable to find Sam. Confused, they didn't know if Sam was lost in the dark, or perhaps had been kidnapped. They called for help and a search was quickly conducted. Sam's body was found about 400 yards from the campsite. The 300-pound black bear that killed Sam was found and killed the next day, after state wildlife officials again sought out the predator in an intensive search involving twenty-six search hounds.

The fatal mauling in Utah was a tragedy. The incident earlier that day had provided clues that a fatal attack may be imminent, but agency managers failed to pick up on those clues. The reality was that an increasingly aggressive black bear, which had demonstrated no fear of humans, had received food rewards. The bear was a ticking bomb. The lack of understanding of the increased danger posed by this bear resulted in the death of a little boy.

A federal court judge called Sam Ives's case "heart-wrenching" as he pondered the details of the little boy's death. US District Judge Dale A. Kimball noted that the boy's parents had "suffered an almost unbearable, unimaginable loss," but that an assignment of fault must be made. Ten percent of the fault fell upon the family itself, the court ruled, because of the food that was found in the family tent (a granola bar and a can of soda). The Utah Division of Wildlife Resources was found to be 25 percent at fault for failing to communicate with the US Forest Service that the wildlife agency had determined the bear was a Level III nuisance that must be destroyed because of the threat to public safety, and because efforts to remove the bear weren't initially successful. The remaining 65 percent of fault was attributed to the United States for its failure to warn the family of the earlier bear attack and failure to close the campsite where the attack had occurred. The federal government was ordered to pay Sam Ives's parents $1.95 million. Additionally, the forest service law enforcement officer who failed to take action or to communicate with others in her agency about the initial attack on Jake Francom was terminated from her position. The court noted that "it was foreseeable that the Francom bear would return to the campsite where it had earlier attacked campers and found food," yet no action was taken to protect the public at that specific location.

It is worth noting that Utah allows bear hunting in this region of the state, but this particular bear apparently had no fear of humans. Utah wildlife officials report that the state's black bear population appears to have increased in the last decade or so, with increased numbers of human-bear conflicts, and rising numbers of bears trapped, moved, and euthanized as a consequence.

Attraction Equals Danger

Black bears are often brought into conflicts with humans after being attracted to human food, garbage, or feed products set out for pets or domestic animals. Without fail, every year in North America humans receive injuries from being mauled by black bears. Researchers believe that black bears can become increasingly aggressive in seeking human-provided food or garbage, which increases the likelihood of serious attacks on humans.

From 1931 to 1969, during the period when bears were allowed to feed in open garbage dumps in Yellowstone National Park, black bears injured an average of forty-five park visitors a year, according to bear managers in the park. Bears had learned to associate humans with food, and had become habituated to the presence of humans. The number of such encounters decreased once the garbage dumps were closed in the national park and officials stepped up efforts to reduce bear-human conflicts. Park records indicate that more than 330 "nuisance" black bears were removed (either killed or placed in captivity) from the population in the ten years after the dumps were closed, and human injuries from black bear attacks dropped to about one or two per year.

California's Yosemite National Park experienced bear issues similar to Yellowstone's. In addition to earthen garbage pits, park managers established artificial feeding stations, places where bears were intentionally fed human food scraps at remote locations, to reduce conflicts between black bears and people in the 1930s, according to a paper written by Joseph Madison, published in *Human–Wildlife Conflicts*. The end result was a very high density of bears in the park,

BLACK BEAR FACTS

Black bears are large predators with a wide distribution in North America. They are found as far south as Mexico, north through Canada and Alaska, and across the United States. There are at least 750,000 black bears in North America—there may be more than 900,000, according to the International Union for Conservation of Nature. Black bears have varied pelage—from blonde to brown, chocolate-colored, and black. Many black bears have brown muzzles and a white-colored triangle on the upper chest.

Just as colorations vary, so do weights of black bears. Mature males in the western states average 250 to 300 pounds in midsummer, and females average about 75 pounds less. Pennsylvania officials recorded a 454-pound female black bear, while Minnesota officials recorded a female that weighed in at 520 pounds. Nevada instituted its first regulated hunting season in 2011, and one male harvested weighed more than 700 pounds, with a chest girth of 64 inches. The largest known wild black bear was an 880-pound male from North Carolina. Weights vary by season, age, and food supply.

Black bears are omnivores, meaning they eat both plants and animals, and most bears are opportunists, eating whatever food source is available in a local area.

and bears learned to break into vehicles looking for food rewards. Their burglaries became widespread and continued to cause problems until the park finally closed the feeding stations and dumps in the 1970s. Yosemite bears that consistently exhibited aggressive behavior toward humans or entered into cabins or tents were killed by wildlife managers, to the tune of about twenty-four bears a year, according to Madison. Agency managers began an intensive program of aversive conditioning to prod the bears back toward natural avoidance of humans and human developments.

The danger posed by fed bears can't be discounted. In August 2009, a black bear killed a seventy-four-year-old woman who officials believe had been feeding wild black bears near her Ouray, Colorado, home for more than a decade. A male bear weighing nearly 400 pounds was found feeding on the woman's body and was shot by a law enforcement officer, as was another bear discovered on the property. The woman had fed the bears dog food and scraps through a metal fence she had constructed around her porch, but one of the animals apparently reached through the barricade and grabbed the woman, killing her. Neighbors had complained about the woman's bear-feeding activities after bears began to break into their homes, apparently seeking the food they were accustomed to receiving from their neighbor.

Various factors in this fatal attack indicated a situation had developed increasing the risk of an attack: the bear's loss of fear of humans, the food rewards received by the bear during its encounters with humans, and the bear's increasingly aggressive behavior. Bear managers repeatedly caution the public that "a fed bear is a dead bear" because of the danger these animals pose, but some members of the public ignore the warnings and feed these big predators anyway, posing risks not just to themselves, but to all their neighbors.

FALL: A SPECIAL TIME OF YEAR

Crisp, cool mornings and shorter days in September signal the end of summer, but these also signal the start of a time of frenzied feeding for black bears and grizzly bears. With winter looming ahead, bears need to consume as many calories and pack on as much weight as possible to sustain them through their winter hibernation. This period of binge eating is called hyperphagia, and bears may spend as many as twenty hours a day eating. A black bear will increase its normal 8,000-calories-a-day intake to 20,000 calories a day. During this time, the combination of hungry bears and careless humans can create conflict situations.

Colorado Parks and Wildlife, for example, cautions that, while black bears don't typically attack humans, "they are large, powerful animals and their determination to eat makes them dangerous when they learn human items and places are a source of food."

During the fall hyperphagia, bears may spend as many as twenty hours a day eating.

When the Bear Doesn't Run Away

Bear behavior varies during human encounters. In some cases, the bear flees. In other cases, the bear may adopt a defensive threat behavior in which it swats the ground with its front paws, loudly clacks its teeth, and bluff charges (charges forward but stops short of making contact). During these defensive behaviors, a bear often vocalizes, with the sounds varying from huffing and snorting to growling. These threat behaviors rarely end with a physical attack, so long as the bear is given plenty of space and doesn't feel further pressured.

Bear behavior varies during human encounters, with the bears sometimes fleeing.

Black bear predatory behavior directed toward humans has little similarity to bear defensive behavior. With predatory behavior, the bear generally does not conduct threatening displays such as teeth clacking, bluff charging, or vocalizations. A black bear in predatory hunting mode will search out, follow, hunt, or stalk the subject of its interest, and will launch into a full assault, slashing with its paws and teeth. A black bear exhibiting predatory behavior may drag its prey (or victim), feed upon it, bury it, or guard it.

Bear attack expert Stephen Herrero of the University of Calgary in Alberta, Canada, led a group of scientists in an examination of fatal black bear attacks on humans, resulting in the publication of a 2011 paper in the *Journal of Wildlife Management*. The paper provided information about the predatory behavior exhibited by these animals, noting that once predatory behavior is initiated, it may persist for hours unless it is deterred. They found that after one person has been killed by a black bear, the bear may attempt or succeed in killing other nearby people. "Such bears appear to be strongly motivated, as if a switch had been thrown," the researchers wrote. "Once a black bear has killed a person, there is an increased chance that it will try to kill other people."

Recent black bear attacks in Tennessee reveal the apparent randomness of some such events—and the terrifying reality when a black bear looks at humans as prey. In May 2000, fifty year old Glenda Ann Bradley was hiking in Great Smoky Mountains National Park and was killed in what wildlife officials called an unprovoked attack. Separated from her hiking partner for a short time while he fished, he came back to find Bradley already dead, with a 112 pound female bear standing over her body, with a yearling cub at its side. The adult bear behaved aggressively and would not back down, and both of the animals fed on the woman's body. About a dozen hikers and campers arrived on the grisly scene and threw rocks at the bear and yelled at it for several hours until park rangers arrived with firearms and killed both bears.

Bears inside national parks are fully protected from persecution, and are not generally subject to human harassment or hunting pressure, so they have little, if any, reason to fear humans. The bear that killed Bradley had previously been captured and marked for research purposes, but it was not known as a nuisance bear, and it was not known to be food-conditioned.

Bear expert Herrero, discussing the bear's clearly predatory behavior in the Tennessee attack, stated, "This stalking behavior is very different from the normal aggressive display of a bear when it wants space." This bear didn't want space—it wanted its meal.

One afternoon in April 2006, a family was mauled by a black bear in Tennessee's Cherokee National Forest. A black bear raced down a ridge to attack a two-year-old boy as the family played in a pool near a waterfall. The mother was mauled and dragged away while saving her son, and was knocked unconscious during the mauling. When paramedics arrived, the mother returned to consciousness long enough to ask about her children, at which point rescuers realized a child was missing. Her six-year-old daughter had become separated from the family during the ordeal, and had been killed by the bear. The bear was later found and killed. Bear experts determined the attack was unprovoked and predatory.

In August 2008, eight-year-old Evan Pala from Florida was on a hiking trail with his father in Great Smoky Mountains National Park when a black bear jumped out of the trees and attacked the boy. The father saw the attack, and in turn launched an attack on the bear, as did the boy's ten-year-old brother. The two managed to pull the bear off Evan, and Evan ran to get away, but stumbled and fell, and the bear pounced again. Evan's father and brother once again pulled the bear off the boy. Eventually all three members of the family escaped the bear, and all three ultimately recovered from their injuries. The bear was later shot by park rangers after it again behaved aggressively by charging them. The bear weighed 86 pounds—just 25 pounds more than Evan. In this case, the park's bear population was protected from human harassment and hunting, and the bear showed no demonstrated fear of humans.

Attacks by Healthy Males Are Most Common

Herrero and his research team examined fatal attacks on humans by black bears from 1900 through 2009. They found at least sixty-three people had been killed by wild black bears during that period. These attacks were not by rabid animals, but instead were inflicted by healthy bears.

During this time, people of all ages were killed by bears, not just the very young, small, or older people, as many would assume. Those killed included both men and women. Although it is assumed that a female black bear with cubs may be more dangerous, in reality, the majority of the fatal attacks on humans involved male bears, and most attacks took place during the daylight hours.

Less than 40 percent of fatal black bear attacks on humans in North America in the last 200 years involved bears that had encountered human food or garbage near the attack site, and few of the bears involved in fatal attacks were known to have a history of association with people. *This indicates the animals may view humans as prey.* It's also worth noting that in none of the fatal encounters during this time period did the victims use bear pepper spray to defend themselves.

Most fatal attacks on humans by black bears involve predatory male bears.

Predatory Attacks Can Be Made by Either Sex

In one of the most disturbing black bear attacks ever recorded, federal geologist Cynthia Dusel-Bacon was mauled while working alone in a remote location in Alaska in August 1977. A black bear erupted out of the brush and came toward Dusel-Bacon, but she stood her ground, shouting loudly at the bear, waving her arms and clapping, being noisy as she tried to scare the bear away. Instead of running away, the bear stalked toward her and attacked. Dusel-Bacon found herself facedown on the ground and played dead. The bear continued to maul the woman and dragged her into the brush, stopping now and then to rest in the 30-minute ordeal. Dusel-Bacon managed to call out on her radio that she needed help, that a bear was eating her. The bear resumed biting her and tore into her backpack for her

A black bear in predatory hunting mode will search out, follow, hunt, or stalk the subject of its interest.

lunch after savagely mauling both her arms. Eventually a helicopter came in for the rescue, frightening the bear away. Dusel-Bacon was unable to move her arms, so all she could do to signal the helicopter that she was alive was kick her legs. She was flown out of the bush and into emergency surgery, but her left arm had to be amputated at the elbow, and her entire right arm was amputated. Dusel-Bacon had other wounds that took a long time to heal, where the bear had eaten her flesh, but eventually she was released from the hospital. This inspiring woman returned to her work for the US Geological Survey after being fitted with artificial limbs.

Although an adult female black bear was found and killed near the attack site, there is doubt that this animal was responsible for the mauling. The circumstances indicate that Dusel-Bacon was the victim of a bear that had viewed a human being as prey. Dusel-Bacon indicated she feels she must have startled the sleeping bear, but once the attack began, the bear intended to eat her. She indeed had become prey.

Multiple Victims

Even though the risk of a fatal black bear attack is low, the risk does exist. Although most black bear attacks involve single individuals being mauled and killed, in 1978, in Algonquin Provincial Park in Canada, three boys (ages twelve to sixteen) were stalked and killed while fishing. A conservation officer participating in the search for the missing boys came upon the bear, which had gathered the bodies into one spot and covered them with debris, feeding on two of the bodies. The officer shot and killed the nearly 300-pound adult male black bear.

A predatory black bear killed two people in northern Alberta in 1980. The man and woman were associated with a drilling rig camp nearby and had separately gone out for walks. The man had gone out alone first, and when he didn't return, the woman and a male companion went out to find him. The couple was attacked by an aggressive black bear, and although the man escaped the attack by climbing a tree and fighting back, the woman was dragged from the tree and killed. Others from the camp arrived on the scene and killed the bear. The body of the male friend they had been seeking out was discovered later, also a victim of the same bear.

The Higher the Number of Bears, the Higher the Risk

Researchers have found a correlation between the number of black bears in an area and the risk of fatal attacks on humans. A greater number of bears means greater risk. Thus, when people have more opportunities to encounter bears, the risk of fatal attacks rises.

Eighty-six percent of fatal attacks on humans by black bears have occurred since 1960, indicating the number of such attacks is increasing. Interestingly, more fatal attacks occurred in Canada and Alaska, even though those areas have a much smaller human population.

Herrero and his fellow researchers speculate that the reason is because Canada has less hunting pressure on its bears, which can influence predatory behavior toward humans.

"With far less hunting pressure, more bold males survive," according to Herrero.

So why aren't even more people killed by black bears? One of the primary reasons is that bears that behave aggressively toward humans, or are involved in attacks on humans, are sought out and killed by wildlife managers. This selective removal helps to eliminate bears with human-aggressive behavior from the gene pool. Just as dog breeders selectively breed dogs to encourage certain characteristics and discourage others, eliminating bears that attack humans from the gene pool may help to "select" against predatory bears.

In June 2010, a black bear attacked a man hiking with his family one afternoon in the Red River Gorge area of Kentucky's Daniel Boone National Forest. Although the man was initially not alarmed when he spotted the bear on the trail behind him, that changed when the bear began deliberately walking toward him. His subsequent attempts to divert the bear's attention—including dropping items on the ground and retreating—failed. The bear was determined, pursuing the man, biting him on the back of the leg as he tried to get behind a tree. The man was engaged in a battle with the bear when other hikers arrived on the scene and came to his aid, yelling at the bear and throwing objects at it until the bear let the man go. The bear did not retreat, but actually followed the group down the trail before finally disappearing into the forest. Officials evacuated the area and closed it to recreational use, but the bear was not found. This bear, which had exhibited predatory behavior toward humans, was reported to be wearing ear tags, indicating wildlife managers had captured and tagged it at some point in the past.

Danger in the Dark

Black bear attacks continue to make headlines in American media, and many of the cases involve bears trying to pull people from their tents in the middle of the night.

In July 2011, a black bear entered a Colorado campground occupied by hundreds of people gathered for a bow-hunting event and tried to grab one of two teenage boys as they slept in a tent. The teenager was able to fight off the bear, although he did receive medical treatment for deep lacerations on one of his legs. State wildlife officials—recognizing the danger of an animal that would enter a tent to attack a sleeping person—used tracking dogs to find the 200-pound adult male black bear, which was then destroyed.

A month later, the *Denver Post* reported on three back-to-back bear attacks on humans southwest of Aspen, Colorado. It started when a black bear damaged an unoccupied tent. A few nights later, a bear injured one of two campers sleeping in a tent in a developed campground. A week later, three campers in separate tents were awoken when a black bear tore into one of the tents and began attacking the man sleeping inside. The man fought the bear off as he yelled for help from the other campers. All three men yelled at the bear, which lingered in the area for an extended period of time. The campers hiked out of the area to get the wounded man medical treatment. State and federal wildlife officials using tracking dogs were able to find and kill the adult male black bear suspected in these three attacks.

It wasn't just black bears in the western states that were causing problems. In that same month (August 2011), a black bear injured two boys as they slept in tents at a youth camp, with a large group of other campers, in a New Jersey state forest. The camp supervisor managed to get all the boys into a building. The bear remained in the area until a state park officer shot it.

Later that fall, a Pennsylvania man was involved in hand-to-paw combat with a black bear that chased his dog inside the family home in the wee hours before dawn. Switching its attention from the dog to the man, the bear and man brawled inside the living room until the man's wife entered the room and was also attacked. The man continued fighting the bear until the bear stopped the attack on him and ran out the open door. Unfortunately, the wife had retreated outside and was once again attacked by the bear. Then, for some reason, the bear stopped the attack. The bear left the area, and the couple did eventually recover from their wounds.

Although most attacks in the summer of 2011 occurred in the dark of night, there were two notable exceptions. In the first case, a seventy-two-year-old Native American woman—a treasured tribal elder—was mauled to death by a black bear outside her home in a remote area of British Columbia in July 2011. Bears had been frequenting her remote property—even attempting to gain entrance to her home—prior to the fatal attack. Tribal officials had determined the animals were problem bears that should be destroyed, but the woman had protested against their destruction. By the time her body was discovered, bears had fed on her remains, and four black bears were killed at the scene in the following days.

The second daytime case in 2011 took place in Arizona. Arizona officials were challenged by a large number of predatory black bear attacks in both 2011 and 2012. In 2011, a sixty-one-year-old woman was walking her dog at a country club northeast of Phoenix when she was attacked by a 250-pound male black bear. Witnesses and motorists saw the attack and used their vehicles to scare the bear away from the initial attack, but the predatory bear returned to maul the victim two more times before she could be rescued. The bear, which had been seen scavenging for food in a dumpster prior to the attack, was tracked and killed by wildlife officials. Sadly, four weeks after being mauled, the woman died from a massive brain hemorrhage resulting from the attack.

Several of the 2012 attacks involved bears attacking humans as they slept. In late May 2012, a seventy-four-year-old Arizona woman was asleep in a tent with her husband and dog in the Ponderosa Campground of the Tonto National Forest, east of Payson, Arizona, when a black bear ripped its way into the tent and clawed at her, leaving her with lacerations on her scalp. She was treated at a local hospital for her injuries and released. A large, adult black bear had been seen around the campsite dumpsters the evening prior to the attack, and had been chased off by the campsite host, only to return early the next morning to seek the woman out in her tent. Federal officials responded to the attack by closing the campground and calling in animal control specialists to track the bear. State wildlife officials acknowledged the bear was a threat to human safety so it had to be lethally removed, but the bear was not found. The campground was reopened two weeks later.

A month after the Ponderosa Campground bear attack, and just one mile away, a twenty-nine-year-old man sleeping on a cot in an uncompleted cabin was startled awake during the night as a black bear pounced on him, biting his leg. The man hollered to his buddy sleeping nearby that something had attacked him. The bear had retreated in response to the commotion, but soon looked back through the open window at the men. The men yelled and chased the bear away, returning to the cabin to go back to sleep, but alerted authorities to the attack the next morning.

A day later, back at the Ponderosa Campground, a bear mauled and injured a thirty-year-old man as he slept in a tent with his girlfriend and her small child. The bear then wandered into a neighboring campsite, where a camper reportedly shot at it with a handgun. The bear was not found. Forest service officials closed three campgrounds and prohibited overnight use in two others in the area, publicly declaring: "We simply cannot ensure camper safety in these areas and need to take more immediate steps to protect the public."

Three black bears were lethally removed from the area, but DNA testing of bear hair samples collected from the attack sites did not provide positive confirmation that any of the animals that were killed were those that had been actually involved in the attacks. State wildlife officials pledged to continue searching for the offending bear or bears, noting, "The offending animals' actions are bold and extremely predatory in nature, and still remain a threat."

Although it appears that the victims involved in the Arizona black bear attacks in 2012 had taken proper safety precautions, Arizona Game and Fish Department officers believe that the bear responsible for the attacks had already been habituated and conditioned to people, and had come to expect to find food or garbage in human-inhabited areas. The result was a human-predatory black bear that mauled three victims. Bear researchers speculate that black bears that become increasingly aggressive in going after human food or garbage have an increased chance of initiating a serious or fatal attack on humans, an assertion that certainly seems to have played out in Arizona in 2011 and 2012.

At 7:30 a.m. on September 14, 2012, a man was sleeping in his tent in Montana's Bob Marshall Wilderness when a black bear jumped on his tent, collapsing it, and then tore through the fabric as it began mauling the man. The man sprayed the bear with pepper spray, ending the attack. The bear remained in the area until a US Forest Service employee and trail crew arrived on the scene and hazed the bear away. A helicopter flew the victim out of the area for medical treatment.

Montana Fish, Wildlife & Parks investigator Brian Sommers noted that the bear "displayed behavior consistent with food conditioning and habituation." The bear was killed about 70 yards from the scene of the attack, as it was in the process of moving back toward the tent where the attack occurred.

"This was a predatory attack by this black bear," Sommers said.

The mauling victim recovered from his injuries. The 185-pound adult male black bear was reported to be in good condition, and pepper spray was evident on the animal's fur.

Maine wildlife officials recorded nearly 900 bear-related complaints in 2012. And while the state does boast the largest population of black bears in the continental United States, this number was more than double from the year before.

Black Bear Complaints Rise as Attacks Continue

In mid-May 2013, Joe Azougar was enjoying breakfast on the porch of his cabin in northern Ontario when a large adult black bear approached, quickly killing Azougar's dog as it played outside. Azougar retreated inside his small cabin, but the bear pursued him in a clearly predatory attack, busting through a window to get inside. Azougar fled outside, but the bear chased and caught him. Although Azougar put up a fight, he was soon weakened by the numerous injuries inflicted by the bear, and by the time two women drove by and witnessed the attack, the bear was dragging a bloodied and limp Azougar into a ditch. The women approached in their vehicle, honking the horn to scare the bear, which released its hold on the man and retreated. The women managed to get the still-conscious Azougar loaded into the vehicle and hurried him to a hospital for treatment of his injuries, from which he recovered. The predatory bear was shot and killed later that day by an official with the Ontario Ministry of Natural Resources.

A month prior, Ontario officials had issued a press release reminding citizens to call 911 if a black bear poses an immediate threat to personal safety by exhibiting threatening or aggressive behavior, such as entering a school yard while school is in session; stalking people and lingering at the site; entering or trying to enter a residence; wandering into a public gathering; or killing pets or livestock and lingering at the site.

The presence of a dog was noted in a second bear attack later that month, but hundreds of miles away. Also in May 2013, a Wisconsin man was attacked by a black bear outside a cabin after attempting to save his dog from the bruin. The man's wife grabbed a shotgun and hit the bear over the head with it. The man and woman escaped into the cabin, but the bear continued to circle the cabin until a sheriff's deputy arrived and killed the animal.

In June 2013, sixty-four-year-old Robert Weaver and his wife had just motored up to the dock outside their cabin on George Lake, located in a remote region of interior Alaska, and had begun walking toward their cabin when they spotted a bear. They yelled at the bear and it moved to the nearby brush, but continued to watch them. When the bear began its attack, Robert Weaver yelled at his wife to run. She escaped into the safety of their cabin, but Weaver was fatally mauled. While a wildlife trooper was investigating the scene, the bear returned, sneaking up on investigators, and the trooper shot and killed the animal at close range. An examination of the bear's stomach contents confirmed that this was the same bear that had killed Weaver. The bear was a healthy older male, weighing about 230 pounds. State officials deemed this a predatory attack—an attack involving an adult bear that pursued humans as prey.

The frequency of such predatory attacks seems to be increasing. In July 2013, an aggressive black bear attacked a man on a Mission,

British Columbia, trail as the man walked during the evening. The bear apparently appeared on the trail at close range; the man turned to run, but the bear grabbed him by the leg. The man pulled himself up on a nearby fence and managed to get over the top. Passing traffic helped to deter the bear, which was still intent on getting to the man, and the animal fled back into the forest.

In August 2013, a twelve-year-old girl was attacked by a black bear as she jogged near her home in Cadillac, Michigan. The girl played dead and the bear eventually left her. When she got up to run, screaming for help, the bear returned, but the girl's neighbors were able to scare it away. The girl received injuries, but recovered from her wounds. State wildlife officials noted their belief that this was an unprovoked attack, and although a black bear was killed a few miles from the attack site, DNA tests revealed it was not the bear responsible for the attack.

Florida closed out 2013 with not just an increase in the number of complaints about black bears in neighborhoods, but also with the most serious black bear attack on a human in the state's history. A fifty-four-year-old woman, who lived in a gated community in central Florida, had just stepped outside her door one early December evening to walk her two dogs when the bear charged her from the bushes nearby. The woman received severe injuries to her head and face as she fought back, and was eventually rescued by neighbors after the bear retreated and the injured woman made her way to a neighbor's doorstep.

Other residents had complained about numerous encounters with bears in the residential area in the weeks leading up to the attack. Some had taken measures to secure garbage and other items that could attract bears, and others carried foghorns to deter bears when sighted. Residents saw bears on a frequent basis, taking photographs and videos. Bears reportedly approached cars and homes, looking in windows and attempting to break inside.

After the attack, state wildlife officials trapped and removed several black bears from the neighborhood before determining that an adult female black bear had been responsible for the attack. They speculated that the sow, a mother with three cubs, could have been a protective mother that attacked because it felt threatened upon

Black bears inflict injuries on humans every year in North America.

encountering the woman. The sow and two of her three cubs were captured and placed into captivity.

Florida's bear population has risen to 3,000 animals, and state law prohibits the killing of black bears in the state, unless the action is necessary to avoid an imminent threat of death or serious bodily injury. It appears that these particular predators—protected from persecution—had lost their fear of mankind, and the result was the eventual attack on a human. Thankfully, the Florida woman survived the attack.

Educating the Public

As bear populations continue to expand into new areas, or into areas that haven't seen bears for decades, wildlife managers are taking aggressive action to educate residents about being "bear wise." State by state, wildlife officials have launched interagency educational campaigns to help residents adjust to life with bears. The programs emphasize removal of items that can serve as bear attractants (from bird feeders to overflowing garbage), and often include encouragement of the use of bear-proof garbage cans in residential areas bears are known to frequent.

But even an educated public may not agree with the need for agency action when it comes to dealing with conflict bears. In some cases, animal advocates protest agency action that results in the killing of bears involved in conflicts. While wildlife managers are faced with trying to protect public safety, members of this same public actively try to hinder that effort. When a female black bear began breaking into numerous homes through doors and windows in New Jersey in the fall of 2012, agency officials determined the animal was dangerous and killed it. Her cubs were captured and placed in a captive wildlife center. Local animal rights activists held a "memorial service" and public protest over the killing of the dangerous bear.

Natural resource agencies have stepped up efforts to reduce potential conflicts between humans and bears.

Bear-human conflicts have become so widespread that various state wildlife agencies are undertaking research projects in an attempt to get a better understanding of the situation, and to develop possible solutions to alleviate conflicts. Preliminary research has provided surprising information about the number of bears in some urban areas. For example, Colorado Parks and Wildlife have been radio-collaring black bears within a six-mile radius of downtown Durango in the southwestern portion of the state. Their efforts have resulted in the tracking of more than 300 bears in a region of high-quality urban bear habitat. With a better knowledge of where bears are roaming, state wildlife managers are able to target educational efforts and create "bear-wise" communities.

With black bear populations in at least forty states (and across Canada and northern Mexico), there are few places where this species faces threats to its existence. With most black bear populations reported as stable or increasing, there is ample opportunity for conflicts between humans and bears as the two species overlap and interact. State wildlife agencies have few management options outside of regulated hunting (where hunting is allowed). Instead, conflict situations often result in the lethal removal of the bear.

Few black bears involved in fatal attacks on humans were known to have a history of association with people.

LESSONS LEARNED FROM THE ATTACKS

Every year, humans receive injuries from attacks by black bears in North America. But there are important findings to draw from the analysis of these attacks, according to Herrero and his colleagues:

1. Smaller parties of only one or two people are more likely to be attacked.

2. People of all ages and sexes are victims of bear attacks.

3. No specific activity is associated with fatal attacks.

4. No one killed in a black bear attack carried bear spray.

5. Many attacks are initiated by black bears associating food with or seeking food rewards from humans.

6. Most fatal attacks are predatory and are carried out by one bear.

7. Male black bears are responsible for most predatory attacks.

8. Most bears that prey on people are selectively removed from the bear population, reducing the risk of such continued behavior in that population.

9. A food-stressed bear may be more likely to attempt predation on humans, although most bears involved in fatal attacks on humans were healthy.

10. There were no recorded cases of a black bear killing a human in defense of an animal carcass.

Avoiding
Black Bear Conflicts

Most fatal attacks on humans by black bears are predatory in nature, meaning that the bears view humans as prey.

You need to take some precautionary measures to avoid conflicts with black bears. Before you go out, gather together a few safety items, such as a whistle or air horn, and a can of bear spray. Have these items readily accessible for outside excursions and learn how to use the bear spray, including understanding its limitations.

The Ontario Ministry of Natural Resources recommends that if you encounter a bear at a distance, stop what you are doing and try to remain calm. Do not panic. Closely watch the bear while slowly backing away. Do not move closer for a better look or photo. Do not try to escape by running, climbing a tree, or swimming away.

In response to a surprise encounter with a human, a black bear may rise onto its hind legs to get a better look at you and to gather your scent, according to Yellowstone National Park bear officials. A bear's behavior can be terrifying, but generally, the noisier a bear is, the more it is warning you. The bear may be salivating, clacking its teeth together, showing its lips, or noisily huffing or exhaling while making loud, moaning sounds. The bear may lay its ears back along its lowered head. It may slap the ground with its front paws, threatening you to back off.

If you are in a position to have a surprise or close encounter with a bear, and it has provided warning signs, you need to respond to these cues. Do not behave aggressively in return. Get your bear spray ready for use, while talking quietly to the bear in a monotone voice and backing away. Do not turn your back to the bear, and don't make direct eye contact with the bear. If you are near a building, car, or other shelter, get inside.

If the bear continues to advance toward you and does not leave even though it has an escape route and ample time, you may be in imminent danger. Bear attacks are rare, but obviously they do occur. A predatory bear may approach you very quietly, as it would with other prey, and may continue to approach you, regardless of the evasive tactic you take.

If a black bear continues to approach you aggressively, yell loudly and wave your arms to make yourself look bigger. If you have another person with you, do this side by side. Be as loud as you can, using whistles or air horns, and throw whatever objects you can at the bear. Spray the bear with pepper spray—the spray is both an attack deterrent and your last resort. Do anything you can to distract the bear at this point.

Black bears often do short, bluff charges in sudden encounters with humans. As soon as the bear starts to charge, stop backing away and stand your ground. If the bear gets close, use your pepper spray on the charging bear.

Start spraying a two-second blast when the bear is between 30 to 60 feet away, holding the can with both hands and spraying from side to side to make a cloud for the bear to encounter. If the bear keeps charging, keep spraying!

If a black bear does attack you, do not play dead. Fight back with every ounce of energy you have—your life depends on it.

Most fatal attacks on humans by black bears involve predatory male bears. If the bear has approached you quietly and intently, it's going to try to kill you. That behavior is predatory, not protective or surprised.

If you are able to leave the area after encountering a bear, be sure to alert other people you meet about the bear's presence and report the encounter to law enforcement authorities.

Bear managers repeatedly caution the public that a fed bear is a dead bear because of the danger these animals pose.

A black bear that has received a food reward from an encounter with a human may seek out humans in the future, anticipating another food reward. Wildlife managers have a creed that "a fed bear is a dead bear" because, generally, once a bear has learned to associate humans with food rewards, the bear will begin seeking out humans for the food benefit. A bear's nose is approximately one hundred times more sensitive than a human's, so a bear can smell food as far as five miles away. Food-habituated bears will break into buildings and vehicles in search of food—whether at a backcountry trailhead or residence. A person who gets in the way of a food-seeking bear can be injured or killed, and the bear making the attack will need to be destroyed to protect future human safety.

If you encounter a black bear, remain calm and slowly back away, giving the bear a clear escape route.

Hiking and Camping Basics

When hiking or camping, never leave trash or leftovers behind. Bears can discover them and begin to associate those trails with food. Follow Leave No Trace ethics. Pack out what you pack in. Food should be safely stored unless it's being prepared for eating or being eaten. Store food, pet food, beverages, and toiletries in airtight containers and coolers, and lock these inside your vehicle. Double-bag trash and place it inside your vehicle, as well. Be sure to roll up all the windows and lock the doors after stashing these items in your vehicle.

Keep a clean tent as well. Aromatic items need to be stored outside the tent. In addition to food, this includes all toiletries, beverages, gum, sunscreen, insect repellant, candles, etc. If you cook at camp, change into clean clothes and store the others in your vehicle. Do your cooking, eating, and dishwashing away from your sleeping area.

In the event storing food inside a vehicle or hard-sided structure isn't an option, food should be suspended in the air out of a bear's reach, which means at least 10 feet clear of the ground and 4 feet horizontally from any supporting tree or pole (see diagrams).

Although many people assume a female black bear with cubs is most dangerous, the majority of fatal attacks on humans involve male bears.

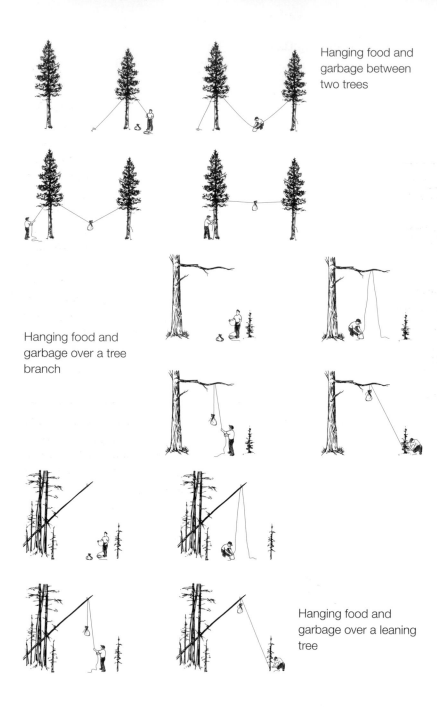

Hanging food and garbage between two trees

Hanging food and garbage over a tree branch

Hanging food and garbage over a leaning tree

ABOUT BEAR SPRAY

Bear spray is a nonlethal pepper spray derived from capsicum, the heat-simulating compound found in chili peppers. Bear spray is an extreme irritant to human or mammal skin, eyes, throat, and lungs. Spraying a charging bear with pepper spray interferes with the animal's ability to breathe and smell, as well as its ability to see clearly, thus stopping the attack and giving you a chance to escape. You don't have to be an excellent shot to be effective with a can of bear spray—a cloud of spray between you and a charging bear should be enough for your immediate retreat from the area.

Bear spray should not be used to spray tents, equipment, or campsites. This does not deter bears and may, in fact, attract bears because of the smell.

Having your can of bear spray stored in a pack on your back with its zip-tie safety strap attached isn't going to help you. Rather, the spray needs to be within easy reach, with the zip-tie removed, and you need to know how to operate it. It's a good idea to practice using your spray and how you would react in a moment of danger. Practice until you can quickly unclip the spray from your belt or holster, flip the safety tab off with your thumb, and fire. Realize that wind will affect the movement of the spray. The more you've practiced, the more self-confidence you'll have should you need to use the spray in a critical moment.

Be aware that cans of bear spray have expiration dates, so be sure to check your can and promptly replace cans with expired dates, or cans that have been affected by freezing temperatures. Outdated, unused, or dented cans of spray are best for practice. Do not go into the field with a used can. A new can of spray with a minimum volume of 7.9 ounces and a spray capacity of at least six seconds is recommended.

Chapter 2
Coyotes

In October 2009, nineteen-year-old folk musician Taylor Mitchell decided to hike in Cape Breton Highlands National Park, in Nova Scotia, Canada—a park known for its spectacular rugged highlands and ocean scenery. Mitchell was on tour and scheduled to perform that evening to promote her new CD, but the Toronto native had set out on the Highline Trail for an afternoon stroll when she was attacked by a pack of three coyotes. Hearing her screams, other hikers came to her rescue, scaring off the one remaining coyote and calling for emergency medical attention. Mitchell later died from injuries sustained in what has been characterized as a predatory attack. Because Mitchell was alone when the attack occurred, no one knows exactly what happened, or what—if anything—may have triggered the attack. One adult male coyote was shot and wounded at the scene of the attack by a Royal Canadian Mounted Police officer. Although the animal ran away after being wounded, it was later killed by wildlife officials. An aggressive female coyote was also killed when it returned to the attack site a few hours later. A second adult male coyote was also believed to have been involved in the attack, based on photographs taken by other people. Shortly before the attack on Mitchell, other hikers in the area had photographed several coyotes up close that showed no fear of humans.

In total, six coyotes were killed in the area near the site of the fatal attack shortly after it occurred and in subsequent weeks. Evidence indicated that three of the six coyotes had been involved in the attack. All three animals were in good physical condition and were healthy, and at least one of the coyotes had fed on its victim. Wildlife officials suspected that these coyotes had become habituated to humans during the tourist season, and this may have involved the animals receiving food rewards from humans.

While Mitchell's was the first confirmed human fatality due to coyote attack in the park, the area where Mitchell hiked has a history of coyote attacks on humans, although most human injuries were mild and involved scratches and bites. The coyote is a relatively new resident of Nova Scotia, recorded there for the first time in 1976 and becoming common since then. Numerous factors indicated an increased risk to humans from coyotes in Cape Breton Highlands National Park, including the observed loss of fear of humans by coyotes and their increasingly aggressive behavior toward humans. Additionally, coyotes are protected in this national park (as they are in all national parks). The animals had no reason to fear or avoid humans, and this coyote pack eventually turned to a human as prey.

Eastern coyotes, such as those found in Nova Scotia where Mitchell was killed, weigh more than their western counterparts, and it appears that the reason for such a size difference is the integration of wolf genetics into the eastern coyote population. The average weight of coyotes in Nova Scotia is about 34 pounds, and 50-pound eastern coyotes are not uncommon. For comparison, adult male coyotes in the southwestern United States, from California or New Mexico, weigh about 24 pounds. Researchers disagree as to the sources of the wolf genetics, with one group claiming the eastern coyote is more accurately termed a "coywolf," which originated through hybridization between eastern wolves and coyotes and now maintains its uniformity between the species, while others assert that the northeastern coyote population is part of a larger coyote population that regularly interbreeds with both coyotes and the population of hybrid coyote/wolves that occur in southern Ontario. Regardless, the result is a larger-than-average coyote.

In the wake of Mitchell's tragic death, the government of Nova Scotia instituted a program to reduce aggressive coyote behavior, including offering a $20-per-pelt incentive for professional trappers to harvest coyotes; training fifteen trappers to target aggressive coyotes; hiring a specialist to work on human/wildlife conflicts; and enhancing education about avoiding coyotes.

"The aggressive coyote situation is a serious issue in many communities, and our decision today is based on all available science and professional experience," said Nova Scotia's natural resources minister John MacDonell. "These new measures are designed to change the behavior of aggressive coyotes so they retain fear and avoid humans." The department also began instituting a new policy requiring immediate action toward animals that behave aggressively toward people.

Most coyotes are associated with packs consisting of six to seven animals Packs defend their territories, and territories are often passed from one generation to the next.

Although the new program was effective at increasing hunting and trapping pressure on coyotes, attacks on humans persist in the area. In the year after the program began in April 2010, there were 104 reports of aggressive coyotes investigated by wildlife officers, including nineteen situations requiring an immediate agency response, which resulted in the killing of thirty coyotes.

HOW ANIMALS RESPOND TO HUMANS

In a 1998 paper, "Understanding Wildlife Responses to Humans," Doug Whittaker and Richard Knight (both of Colorado State University) described how wildlife behavior experts classify wildlife responses to humans, noting they fall into three general categories: attraction, habituation, and avoidance.

Attraction occurs when an animal experiences positive reinforcement and moves toward humans or human-supplied stimuli. Examples include animals learning to raid garbage cans for food rewards, or animals that seek out human settlements for shelter or security.

Habituation is defined as a waning response to repeated neutral stimuli, typically resulting in the loss of avoidance or escape responses. The neutral part is important—a bear that is attracted to humans because of expected food rewards is not habituated, but a bear that continues to graze on vegetation alongside the highway in Yellowstone National Park, despite the presence of hundreds of tourists and their vehicles inching ever closer, is habituated.

Whittaker and Knight noted in their paper that "Wildlife are capable of becoming habituated to people, human-made environments, and most any human stimuli."

Avoidance is the aversion to negative consequences associated with a stimulus (the opposite of attraction).

While some of these behaviors may be learned, others may have genetic or cultural components within animal populations.

Cape Breton Attacks Continue

The attacks on humans continue in Cape Breton. In August 2010, a coyote attacked a sixteen-year-old girl while she was sleeping outside in a sleeping bag as the other members of her family slept in a nearby tent. The teenage girl managed to fight off the animal but received several bites to her head.

In May 2012, a fourteen-year-old boy stepped off his motorcycle on a trail in Cape Breton Regional Municipality and was viciously attacked by a coyote that knocked him to the ground and repeatedly bit him. The coyote reportedly bit the boy's feet before attacking the area behind his knee. Fortunately, the teenager was wearing protective safety gear designed for dirt biking, including a chest protector and padded pants, so the coyote was unable to penetrate much of his clothing. The boy did receive injuries to his leg and buttock. The teenager aggressively responded to the attack, grabbing the coyote by the throat until he could get back on his feet, at which point he continued kicking the animal (with his hard-toed motorcycle boots) until the coyote retreated.

The puzzler of why coyotes have become so aggressive in Cape Breton prompted Parks Canada officials to put up $100,000 in 2012 for a two-year research project aimed at answering that question, and at developing a protocol for aversion techniques that could be used on coyotes. Preliminary results are due in 2014.

Parks Canada also began a campaign to train coyotes in the area to once again fear humans. Parks Canada's resource conservation manager Derek Quann stated: "Coyotes live in family groups, and their learning is social learning, which leads to multi-generational behavior. Coyotes are now being raised as pups not to fear people." Agency officials are therefore working to recondition the predator population to fear humans.

EASTERN COYOTES

Although coyotes evolved as hunters of small prey, recent evolutionary changes see the animals becoming larger and turning to larger prey species, such as deer. Genetic evidence suggests that coyotes began expanding their range as wolf populations were decimated in the 1800s, colonizing the northeastern portion of the United States and eastern Canada. As the coyote population expanded into new areas, the animals encountered remnant wolves, and hybridized with wolves in the Great Lakes region. There is also some evidence of hybridization with dogs, so eastern coyotes today are of a mixed background, but have evolved into a distinct ecological unit—both physically and behaviorally.

Members of the eastern coyote population are larger than their western counterparts, but are smaller than wolves. Examination of the skulls of eastern coyotes show more than size differences from their western relatives; the examination suggests the wolf's genetic influence, such as "strong bite forces and resistance to the mechanical stresses imposed by large, struggling prey," according to a paper authored by scientists with the USDA National Wildlife Research Center.

The National Wildlife Research Center reports that eastern coyotes currently have adverse impacts on certain wildlife populations, including white-tailed deer. Coyotes also reportedly threaten the recovery of the endangered red wolf through hybridization, and are also impacting an endangered population of caribou.

Attacks in the United States

Although many coyote attacks have resulted in human injury, Taylor Mitchell's death is the second death attributed to coyote attack (and the first in Cape Breton park). In 1981, a coyote killed three-year-old Kelly Keen; she was attacked in the front yard of her home in Glendale, California. In the eighty days after the attack, wildlife control specialists removed fifty-five coyotes from within a half mile of the attack site. Three other small children were attacked and bit by coyotes in a community 90 miles away that same month.

Places like national parks pose near-perfect scenarios for conflicts between people and coyotes. Coyote populations may expand in association with human development and the food base provided (either intentionally or unintentionally), and these areas draw large numbers of people. It is inevitable that the two species will interact and, in some cases, come in conflict.

Yellowstone National Park experienced numerous coyote attacks on humans in the 1990s. In January 1990, a Chicago man was cross-country skiing near the Old Faithful Geyser in Yellowstone when he

Coyote pairs may return to and use the same natal dens to have their pups. Research indicates that coyotes today are still using dens that were actively used by coyotes in the 1940s in Yellowstone National Park.

came upon a coyote lying in the trail. Before the man could stop, the coyote lunged at his face, biting him and knocking him to the snowy ground. The man fought back, hitting the coyote with one of his skis, and managed to get away. The man received medical treatment for the numerous bites and scratches to his face, arms, and body. When rangers arrived at the attack site, they were greeted by not just one but two aggressive coyotes, both of which they shot and killed. These coyotes were already known to National Park Service officials as having shown aggression toward people, including inflicting minor injuries, presumably after receiving food rewards from previous human contact.

In one case in the mid-1990s, a German man hiking with another person in Yellowstone stopped to rest in a field and ended up falling asleep. He woke with a sharp pain in his foot—a coyote had bitten him. The coyote circled the two people for a moment before departing. The man received treatment for minor injuries, and a ranger returned to the scene of the attack to observe the animal. The coyote attempted to attack the ranger. The coyote was subsequently captured and killed, and later tested negative for rabies and distemper.

Park service officials developed a program of scaring unwary coyotes from visitor use areas with cracker shell rounds, bear-repellent spray, and other aversive conditioning techniques, but saw little indication that such methods caused long-term changes in coyote behavior. In response, park policy was changed and focused on relocation or removal of problem coyotes.

The coyote has gradually expanded its range in the last century, seeming to thrive in the presence of human populations and human development. Once restricted to the central part of North America, coyotes are now found across the continent, from north to south and from coast to coast. They are found in every major ecosystem in North America, from wilderness and national parks to agricultural and industrial zones, and in every major city in the country. If you live in the United States, coyotes probably inhabit your neighborhood.

Coyotes are highly adaptable animals, preying on mice, rabbits, and ground squirrels one week, human garbage and dog food the next. They will eat carrion, kill lambs and young deer, and prey on neighborhood pets. In areas where coyotes learn to associate human presence with food, the small predators lose their fear of humans and become bold or aggressive. Coyotes now thrive in close proximity to people and have benefitted from human alterations to the environment.

While human deaths due to coyote attacks are rare, nonfatal attacks on humans by coyotes are not, and have been increasing. California records about a dozen coyote attacks on humans each year. Researchers believe that, in the absence of harassment by humans, coyotes lose their fear of humans.

Colorado Parks and Wildlife has had ample experience in dealing with urban coyotes and recommends: "It is imperative that communities work together to instill the healthy and natural fear of humans back into coyotes—for their health and safety and ours. Coyotes are quick learners and consistent negative experiences can teach them to avoid people."

Most coyote attacks on humans occur during pup-rearing season (May through August).

Although conflicts occur year-round where coyotes and humans come into contact, most conflicts occur during the coyote breeding season, which is generally February and March, and during pup-rearing season. Coyote pups are born about two months after the breeding season, so the food requirements for the growing young and the nursing female remain high until late in the summer. This tends to be the time when people and their pets spend more time outdoors, so the possibility of coyote encounters, and conflicts, increases during this time as well.

Residential areas provide all the habitat components for coyotes—food, water, and sheltered cover. Yard landscaping provides brushy areas for the small mammals that coyotes prey on, and there is plenty of open space and water in municipal parks, yards, and trails. Food sources are nearly unlimited.

Types of Coyote Attack

In December 2013, a Summerland, British Colombia, woman was walking a friend's dog along a well-used community trail when three coyotes approached and surrounded the pair. The woman crouched down over the dog and sustained wounds to her hands and arms as she slapped at the coyotes and protected the dog from harm. This type of attack is classified as a pet-oriented attack—one of five general attack categories delineated by Ohio State University researchers Lynsey White and Stanley Gehrt in a 2009 paper in *Human Dimensions of Wildlife*. In a pet-oriented attack, a person is bitten while trying to rescue a pet from a coyote attack, or the pet may have served as an attractant to the coyote.

In rabid attacks, the offending coyote is identified, captured, and killed, and a positive rabies test confirms the presence of the disease.

A defensive attack involves a coyote that is accidentally cornered or is defending its pups or a den site.

The final two categories result from the animal losing its fear of humans:

- **Predatory**: The animal (or pack) directly attacks, bites, and in some cases tries to drag a victim away. These cases usually involve severe injuries.

- **Investigative**: A coyote becomes accustomed to its victim and "tests" the victim as a source of possible prey. In these cases, the victim is usually sleeping or resting.

Rabies does not play a critical role in the occurrence of coyote attacks. Few coyotes involved in attacks on humans test positive for rabies.

White and Gehrt recorded 142 coyote attacks on humans, with 159 victims, from 1960 to 2006. These attacks occurred in fourteen states and four Canadian provinces. Nearly half of the attacks happened in California.

Most of the attacks were classified as predatory (37 percent), followed by investigative (22 percent). Predatory attacks are typified by a coyote running straight at its chosen victim, and maintaining the attack even after being discovered by the victim. Although 24 percent of the attacks were categorized as an unknown type, attacks by rabid animals constituted 7 percent of the total, with 6 percent classified as pet-related attacks, and the remaining 4 percent classified as defensive.

Most predatory coyote attacks on humans take place during the daylight hours.

Although coyotes attacked people of all ages, the overall percentage of coyote attacks on children was only slightly higher than attacks on adults. In predatory attacks, the majority of attacks were on children ages ten years old or younger. Most attacks occurred during the coyote pup-rearing season. In 75 percent of the cases involving children, the children were playing outside in their yards or driveways before the attack. Coyotes may have viewed the children as prey and were stimulated to attack by children running or behaving in a playful manner, White and Gehrt reported.

Coyotes were provided food—either intentionally or accidentally—by residents near the attack site prior to the attack in 30 percent of the 142 attacks tallied by researchers.

Wild coyotes living in areas where coyote hunting or other predator-control activities take place tend to be active at night and seek hiding places to avoid humans during the day. The large number of attacks that occurred during daylight hours suggests that the offending coyotes were no longer avoiding humans. One study of coyote–human conflicts in national parks in the United States found that aggressive coyote behavior was exhibited most often when coyotes had been receiving food, whether accidentally or intentionally.

Predicted Changes in Behavior

Coyote experts, led by the University of California's Robert Timm and Rex Baker, developed a list of predictable changes in coyote behavior that indicate an increased risk to human safety. These seven escalating steps, which were published in a 2004 paper, are considered the definitive behavioral prediction for an increase in risk of conflicts that may result in coyote attacks on humans.

1. Increased observations of coyotes on streets and in yards at night.

2. Increase in coyotes approaching adults and killing pets at night.

3. Early morning and late afternoon observations of coyotes on streets, in yards, and in parks.

4. Coyotes observed chasing or killing pets during daylight hours.

5. Coyotes attacking and killing pets on leashes or in close proximity to their owners, and coyotes chasing joggers, bicyclists, and other adults.

6. Coyotes observed near children's play areas, such as parks and school grounds, during midday.

7. Coyotes acting aggressively toward adult humans during midday.

Timm and Baker noted: "As coyotes continue to adapt to suburban environments and as their populations continue to expand and increase throughout North America, coyote attacks on humans can be expected to occur and to increase. To reverse this trend, authorities and citizens must act responsibly to correct coyote behavior problems before they escalate into public health and safety risks for children and adults."

In addition to the human safety risk associated with human-habituated coyotes, the presence of coyotes in close association with humans and their pets poses health risks as well. Both humans and pets could be put at risk for rabies and other diseases and parasites that have serious health effects.

Scientists believe that among the factors leading to an increase in predatory coyote attacks are growth in both human and predator populations, as well as the protection of predators that were once harassed by humans.

"Reduced coyote control efforts by federal and/or county agencies, as well as by landowners, may have led to increased coyote attacks in two ways: local coyote numbers are no longer suppressed, and coyotes' fear of humans is no longer reinforced by lethal control efforts (i.e., shooting and trapping)," according to Timm and Baker.

Reductions in sport hunting and target shooting have correlated with a reduction in the wariness of coyotes as a result of a failure to receive negative consequences from human contact.

Predators that are able to exploit the additional food resources available in urban habitats often exhibit higher population densities in urban environments compared with rural areas. For example, more than 5,000 coyotes live within the city limits of Los Angeles— an average of nearly 11 coyotes per square mile. Increased population density, along with an increased survival rate as the animals are protected from hunting, comes with an increased risk of conflict with human neighbors. Some researchers have indicated that the coyote may be the most dangerous carnivore to humans because of its large body size, its potential to hybridize with wolves, and its close association with urban areas.

Coyotes form pair bonds that may last for several years, but not necessarily for life.

Factors Leading to Conflict

Researchers Robert Schmidt and Robert Timm identified factors that may lead to conflicts between humans and coyotes. That list, as outlined in a 2007 paper, included:

- *Resource-rich suburban environments*: Many residential landscapes include lush vegetation that provides excellent habitat for coyote prey species such as rabbits and rodents, which will, in turn, attract coyotes. Bird feeders and pet food are also potential attractants for coyotes.

- *Human acceptance of coyote presence*: Rather than allowing coyotes to come near humans with no negative response, humans need to be proactive. Harassing or hazing coyotes, making threatening gestures, yelling, squirting the animals with water hoses, or throwing rocks at them helps coyotes maintain their wariness around humans.

- *Lack of knowledge of coyote behavior*: Few people realize that coyotes are a plentiful and widespread species, that human-habituated coyotes are very dangerous animals, and that aggressive management actions are needed to intervene before human injuries are sustained. In most cases, lethal control of aggressive individual coyotes is the most effective approach.

- *Feeding of coyotes*: Coyotes can come into conflict with humans as the result of intentional feeding. It only takes one person providing food for coyotes to pose a risk to the health and safety of humans and pets in an entire neighborhood.

- *Reduction in predator control*: Once individual coyotes demonstrate aggressive/habituated behavior, coyote specialists recommend the animals be removed from the population to prevent attacks. The selective removal of a few bold coyotes helps to restore the fear of humans into the entire coyote population of an area. Wildlife officials recommend that, while coyotes may provide an enjoyable wildlife viewing experience, hikers should keep their distance and not approach the animals.

Suburban and Urban Issues

Coyote attacks on humans are increasing in some suburban areas of the United States. Arizona officials note that there have been eight coyote bites in ten years in Maricopa County, home of capital city Phoenix and nearly four million people. The Denver, Colorado, metropolitan area has been plagued by coyote conflicts in recent years, with twenty coyote bites confirmed between 2000 and the fall of 2011.

The Denver-area suburb of Broomfield experienced a series of coyote attacks on children in 2011. It began in July 2011, with a father strolling on a walking path near his home with his two small children. While the father was putting his little girl into a wagon, his two-year old son ran ahead about 10 feet, and a coyote lunged out from the tall grass and attacked the boy, biting him on the back and buttocks. When both father and son yelled, the coyote ended the attack and retreated a short distance. A juvenile female coyote was killed in the area a few days later.

A few weeks later, a coyote approached a four-year-old girl as she exited a slide on a playground where she was playing with other children. The coyote was intent on the child, approaching within 2 feet when a mother intervened, scaring the animal away.

Two weeks later, the target was a six-year-old boy, in a location less than 100 yards from the playground incident. The playground and pool area were busy with families and children, and several people noticed a coyote in the thick vegetation along the stream corridor. One woman was following the coyote and taking photos with her cell phone camera when a father and his two small children began making their way that direction, with the little boy running ahead. The woman yelled that there was a coyote, but at the same time, the coyote jumped a retaining wall, landing on the boy and biting him. The coyote aggressively postured and snarled at the father before retreating. The animal remained in the area, and local and state officials decided to step up control actions to stop the attacks.

Although hunting is prohibited in the Broomfield area, state wildlife officials killed nearly a dozen coyotes in the neighborhood after the attacks. Local officials instituted a program to reduce vegetation along paths and trails in the community to reduce hiding cover for predators, and city workers began an active campaign to harass and haze any coyotes behaving unacceptably, or using areas that the public generally deemed socially unacceptable for coyote occupancy (such as near schools and playgrounds). A few weeks after the second attack, a coyote attacked a three-year-old girl, again near the same playground. After this final incident, wildlife officials killed an adult male coyote, red in coloration. Officials believed this coyote was responsible for all four incidents, and after its death, there were no further attacks.

Coyotes observed near children's play areas during midday predict an increased risk of impending attack.

The investigation report for the Broomfield conflicts, written by a panel of experts on coyote conflicts including Stan Grant, Julie Young, and Seth Riley, stated: "The 2011 incidents conformed to typical predatory attacks that have been reported in other cities. The similarities of the Broomfield incidents to most predatory attacks in other cities include: children as victims, minor bite wounds, most attacks during daylight, and the attacks occurred in residential areas, including backyards. Finally, a healthy coyote(s) presumably carried out the Broomfield incidents, which is typical of predatory attacks. There was no evidence of disease, starvation, or other types of stress that provoked the attacks."

The report suggested the possibility that the predatory behavior initiated by the coyote or coyotes was stimulated by the movement and sounds of the children prior to the attack (as in the sounds the children made while playing, walking, or running).

Boulder, Colorado, officials were forced to kill an aggressive coyote in late 2011 after the animal repeatedly chased bicycle commuters on a well-used trail. The coyote bit the tire on one bike, and the attacks escalated over a month's time. A ranger responding to a complaint witnessed potentially dangerous behavior as the coyote followed hikers using the trail; the ranger soon thereafter dispatched the animal. Three months later (in February 2012), two additional Boulder coyotes had to be killed after one of them attacked a jogger using a bike path. The jogger received treatment for injuries sustained in the attack.

In June 2012, southern California experienced a series of coyote attacks, one involving a woman who was bitten by a coyote as she was gardening in her gated community. A federal animal damage control agent later killed the coyote. Less than two weeks later, another woman was "bumped" on a leg by a coyote while taking her morning walk, and another coyote was subsequently killed for its apparent lack of fear of humans.

Just a few days later, a five-year-old girl was bitten by a coyote while walking with her family in a state park in Oregon. Other recreationists reported encounters with an aggressive coyote in the same area.

Western states are not alone in experiencing increasing conflicts with coyotes. Residents of Fairfield, Connecticut, suffered from a rash of pet-killing behavior by their local coyote population in July 2012. Coyotes killed at least six dogs in that town.

According to a press release issued by the city of Rye, New York, at 9:15 p.m. on June 25, 2010, a six-year-old girl was in the front yard of her home playing with several other girls when two coyotes ran from a nearby wooded area, jumped on her, and knocked her to the ground. The girl was bitten on her shoulder and thigh, and sustained scratches on the head, back, and neck. The coyotes fled when an adult approached.

Four days later, at 7:15 p.m., a three-year-old girl in the same community was attacked. The girl was playing with a six-year-old neighbor in the yard between their homes, with her father nearby on the deck. A coyote surged out from behind a rock, jumping on the girl and knocking her to the ground. She was bitten on the left side of her neck and torso, and once again the coyote fled when adults came to the rescue.

Reports of coyotes in the city had increased in recent months, and one small dog had been killed by a coyote in an incident leading up to the attacks on the little girls. City officials had been working with a nuisance animal control firm prior to the attacks, and nine coyotes (an adult female and her eight pups) had been captured and relocated. The coyotes responsible for the attacks were not located, and although local law enforcement officers fired shots at several coyotes, they were uncertain whether those shots connected.

As researcher Stanley Gehrt observed, urban areas have an abundance of food for coyotes, and no hunting and trapping. He told the *New York Times*: "It's not just us encroaching on their territory. They're encroaching on us."

Dozens of pets were reported killed by coyotes in Huntington Beach, California, in late 2012, but town officials declined to take action, despite more than 200 calls to town officials about coyotes within just a few months. In addition to the loss of pets, residents reported brazen behavior, including coyotes approaching people. Apparently unaware that the complaints from residents revealed a pattern of escalating behavior indicating an increasing risk of attack on humans, a town councilwoman replied that people needed to modify their behavior to prevent the animals from becoming problems.

Metropolitan areas across the country are experiencing life with coyote populations within city limits, too—from Seattle, St. Paul, and Chicago to Boston, Atlanta, New York City, and Washington, DC.

Researchers estimate anywhere from a few hundred to a couple of thousand coyotes living in the Chicago area alone, home of a long-term study of urban coyotes. Two coyotes were photographed hanging around Wrigley Field on a busy Saturday night in 2012. Conflicts occurred, as expected, and in early 2013, a pack of four snarling coyotes chased a homeowner's dogs into their home 10 miles west of downtown Chicago. The coyotes tried to enter the house, smashing the glass panels on the doors in the process. The homeowner grabbed a BB gun and hit two of the animals, causing the pack to retreat.

Outdoors enthusiasts in the area around Boulder, Colorado, once again had to face aggressive coyotes in late 2012 and early 2013. The first reports were of a woman using a stick to repeatedly hit an aggressive coyote interested in the dog she was walking, and of a coyote lunging at a bicyclist who repeatedly yelled and kicked at the animal. The next report was of an adult woman jogger confronted by one coyote, and then a second coyote behind her. At first, the woman held her own, yelling at the animals, but eventually she ran and was attacked from behind, receiving a bite to her calf. A man saw the attack and came to the jogger's aid, and the two people were eventually able to chase the aggressive coyotes away. The woman received medical treatment at a local hospital.

Within days, more aggressive encounters were reported, including another bicyclist being chased. The city of Boulder held a planning session to develop a coyote management plan, with the intent of reducing the likelihood of future conflicts between humans and coyotes in the problem area of the city. The plan focused on increasing staff presence in the conflict area, increasing public education, and the opportunistic hazing of habituated coyotes. The hazing program involved staff members being present on local trails every day, looking for coyotes and employing techniques designed to scare the animals away from humans.

The first day of implementation of a new month-long program to actively haze coyotes proved the need for such a program. A man walking a dog was approached by an aggressive coyote, with ears back and bared teeth, at the same time a city staffer was hazing away a coyote in an area nearby. To further complicate matters, city officials discovered discarded human food in the area where the problem coyote behavior was reported, indicating the coyotes had received food rewards associated with humans. Educational efforts increased, and the proactive hazing continued.

Unfortunately, despite best efforts by the city of Boulder, conflicts continued. A month after the hazing program ended, two coyotes surrounded a man with two five-year-old boys on the Boulder Creek Path. When one of the boys ran to the man, one of the coyotes lunged at him, biting the child on the back of the leg. The man gave a detailed description of the two coyotes involved, and wildlife officials shot and killed both the animals within the next few days. Within a few weeks, at least two separate incidents of people confronted by aggressive coyotes as they walked their dogs were reported.

Predatory attacks on humans by coyotes usually involve more severe injuries than other types of attacks.

Surging Conflicts in Canada

Canada has also experienced a surge in conflicts between humans and coyotes. An October 2009 video of an aggressive coyote was posted on YouTube.com. The video focuses on a man in northern British Columbia as a coyote approaches him, seemingly in a playful manner at first, and getting more and more aggressive as the encounter continues. The coyote eventually bites and gnaws on the man's boots before the man tires of the encounter and has to aggressively force the animal away. The man engaged in very dangerous behavior, and with the encounter ending in no negative consequence for the coyote, the danger for the next person to encounter the animal is imminently higher.

A woman walking her small dogs on the Highlands Golf Course in Edmonton, Alberta, in October 2012 was startled when a coyote grabbed one of her dogs. When others arrived on the scene, they found the coyote circling and following the woman as she held a second dog in her arms. The coyote was apparently targeting the small dogs as a food source. Although the woman had managed to protect one dog, the other was not recovered. Another dog walker in the area said he had been stalked by a coyote moments before. Both people reported the coyote had refused to retreat when confronted. City officials estimate there are more than 2,000 coyotes in this metropolitan region, and city officials have instituted an educational program focused on avoiding conflicts between humans and coyotes.

Toronto, Canada, officials killed two aggressive coyotes in separate incidents in early 2012. In one case, two young girls were chased by coyotes from a residential yard into a residence, with an eight-year-old girl receiving a bite on her leg in the process. An officer responding to the complaint was confronted by a coyote on a nearby trail and subsequently dispatched the animal. A few months later, during an active law-enforcement investigation, another officer encountered an aggressive coyote just east of Toronto's downtown area and was able to shoot and kill the animal. Toronto officials were forced once again to kill an aggressive coyote after its repeated encounters with people in downtown Toronto in early 2013.

Female coyotes have one estrus cycle per year, so breeding takes place during this time (between January and March).

In March 2013, Parks Canada issued a warning to the public to watch out for a bold coyote in the Lake Louise ski area. The coyote repeatedly approached people and had no fear of humans. The warning included the suggestion that skiers and snowboarders should travel in groups, and children should not be allowed to ski alone.

ANIMAL ADVOCATES PROTEST

Some animal advocates protest when coyotes are killed after aggressive encounters, and fear that government agencies take control too far. In early 2013, the Beach Coyote Coalition in Toronto advocated for peaceful co-existence with coyotes, but in the process discounted or minimized conflicts. It provides dangerously erroneous information. The group insists that coyotes "do not predate on dogs"—a blatantly false statement. Another false statement made by the group is this: "A coyote will not see a person as potential prey."

Rather than notifying wildlife authorities of coyote encounters, the group recommends it be contacted instead: "We recommend that, apart from disclosing the location of the sighting to us, you keep that information confidential in order to protect the coyote." While the group may be well intentioned in its animal advocacy, protecting coyotes that exhibit predatory behavior could result in the loss of human life, or cause severe human injury.

Immediate action should be taken with coyotes that behave aggressively toward people.

Continued Conflict, Injuries, and Debate

A coyote attacked a female security guard working at the entrance to the Kennecott Utah Copper mine outside of Salt Lake City, Utah, in October 2012. The woman was working in the booth when the coyote entered and lunged at her. She defended herself, throwing up her arm, and was bitten several times. The woman was able to get the coyote out of the booth and call for help. A police officer responded to the scene and shot the coyote. The animal was healthy and did not have rabies.

In October 2012, a fourteen-year-old boy was attacked by a coyote he encountered on a trail near his home in Austin, Texas, after neighbors reported aggressive coyotes in the area. The coyote responsible for knocking him to the ground and scratching him was not found, and the boy underwent a series of precautionary rabies shots.

In December 2012, a Kent, Washington, man reported that, while he was out in his backyard with his dog, a pack of three coyotes attacked him. He fought off the animals and also received rabies shots after visiting an emergency room for treatment of his coyote bite and scratches.

In January 2013, a coyote attacked and bit two teenage students while on the Brandeis University campus in Waltham, Massachusetts. One student was walking when the animal approached her from behind, biting her leg. Since the injury did break the skin, the student received medical treatment, including shots for tetanus and rabies. The other student was unharmed in the attack, as her thick boots prevented the coyote from inflicting damage to her skin. City officials reported their belief that someone was feeding the coyote, causing the human aggression.

The city of Waltham posted a notice on its website, noting: "MA Wildlife and the Environmental Police are aware of the situation. It is believed someone is feeding the animal. This has led to it approaching people and grabbing at legs and feet in an attempt to get people to feed it, causing minor abrasions to one Brandeis student."

Although city officials suspected the coyote was aggressive because it had received human food rewards, the notice actually discounted the danger when it continued: "Had the intent been to attack, any injuries would have been quite severe, so people should not fear that a coyote is going around attacking people. However, this is still not acceptable behavior and the public safety is our utmost concern." In reality, the fact that this coyote had already bitten several people should have been cause for alarm, and reason enough to suspect another attack could be imminent, and could be more severe for the next victim.

Waltham could have taken a page out of the playbook of another Massachusetts town. Just a few months before the attacks in Waltham, the Massachusetts town of Belmont's Board of Health approved a coyote management plan that included the deployment of a team of trained volunteers to harass coyotes that grew too bold, and to educate town citizens about how to keep the animals at bay.

Orlando, Florida, residents were disturbed about the number of family pets gone missing from their neighborhoods in early 2013. One man kicked a coyote off the family dog, while a woman screamed when a coyote tried to attack one of her dogs. The coyote fled, but killed the dog in the next yard on its way out. Some neighborhoods tried to hire trappers to help control the problematic predators, but other residents protested, pleading for people to coexist with the animals.

Coyotes may live longer in captivity, but the oldest known wild coyote on record lived fifteen-and-a-half years.

May 2013 saw a spate of coyote attacks on humans throughout the West. Residents of Santa Clarita, California, were warned about an aggressive coyote in their neighborhood after a coyote attacked and killed a small dog as it was being walked on a leash by a child and her mother in Summit Park. A jogger in the same area reported being chased by a coyote a few days later; a passerby came to her aid.

In Kamloops, British Columbia, a man sleeping under the stars in his sleeping bag in a developed campground was attacked by a coyote. The man received stitches, and the coyote—which was in good health and showed no fear of humans—was destroyed by wildlife officers.

Two preschool children were attacked by coyotes in separate incidents on the same day in a busy city park in Colorado Springs, Colorado. Unfortunately, these weren't the first coyote attacks here: There had been other incidents involving aggressive coyotes approaching humans in the area before the attacks. Wildlife officials took action and sought to destroy the coyotes. Two coyotes killed in the area were found to have mange. Some speculate that a wild animal suffering from ill health is more prone to seek out nontraditional prey (such as pets or humans).

In July 2013, a two-year-old girl was bitten and nearly dragged away by a coyote while with her family visiting an Orange County, California, cemetery. The child's mother grabbed the child in a momentary tug-of-war with the coyote and recovered the girl, who then received treatment for her injuries. Although wildlife officials eventually destroyed three coyotes near where the attack took place, a lawsuit was filed against cemetery officials later that fall by a woman who claimed to have been attacked by a coyote while visiting her mother's grave in August. The lawsuit alleged negligence and premised liability due to the cemetery's lack of preventative measures to keep such attacks from happening, as well as a failure to warn visitors of the risk of attack.

While it seems the majority of the attacks are aimed toward children, adults—particularly adult males—are not immune. In October 2013, a twenty-two-year-old Colorado man was attacked by a pack of three coyotes early one morning as he walked away from his disabled car in Niwot. He fought the animals off. Colorado Parks and Wildlife officials called the attack unprovoked and killed three coyotes in the area. Necropsies revealed the animals (two females and one male) to be healthy adults, all with food in their stomachs.

Colorado wildlife officials cautioned: "Coyote attacks on humans are rare; however, coyotes in the metro area become habituated to human presence. Habituation can cause coyotes to lose their healthy and natural fear of people, become territorial, and sometimes aggressive."

Management Challenges

Wildlife managers face a variety of challenges as predator populations expand. According to authors David Foster, Glenn Motzkin, Debra Bernardos, and James Cardoza in a paper published in the *Journal of Biogeography* called "Wildlife Dynamics in the Changing New England Landscape," the trend "towards a maturing forest landscape with large mammals, in conjunction with an expanding suburban and exurban human population, will lead to increasing conflicts between human interests and appreciation for wild nature. At the very least this raises the need for educating humans about wildlife, nature, and its history, and then using this education effectively to modify human behavior and attitudes. In the case of many of the larger mammals (e.g., bear, moose, beaver, coyote), the social carrying capacity of the landscape (i.e., the density and distribution of a species that humans can tolerate or accommodate) is ironically declining as the natural carrying capacity of the land is increasing." After decades of learning about the need to conserve wildlife, it will take a major shift in public thinking to acknowledge that many wildlife (and predator) populations have reached the point that efforts must now turn to keeping a distance from the animals, for the good of both human and animal populations.

The second challenge, of course, is effective regulation of wildlife populations, which Foster and his fellow authors called "a formidable task for a suburbanized human population that is generally poorly informed about nature and wildlife dynamics and is largely opposed to the most ready means of wildlife regulation: hunting and trapping."

Lethal control targeted at individual animals is often the fastest and most effective way to prevent further attacks when a dangerous situation is discovered. An assessment of the Broomfield, Colorado, coyote conflicts found that lethal removal of problem coyotes via high-powered rifle is both a practical and selective method to end conflicts in urban settings. While using a predator call to attract coyotes to an area of repeated conflict often enables offending animals to be removed via lethal control, coyotes are intelligent animals and will likely learn which trucks and people to avoid if a shot is missed or the animal is harassed before a shot can be taken.

Rather than publicly condemning wildlife officials for taking needed action to reduce dangers to the public in neighborhoods experiencing conflicts between humans and coyotes, it would be helpful for residents to understand and be supportive of the need for action when aggressive coyotes are identified in a community. Once coyotes behave in a bold or aggressive manner around humans, it is unlikely that attempts at hazing will ultimately be successful in reversing the problem. In these circumstances, removal of the offending animal is the only effective strategy.

Removal of a few problem coyotes can help to reestablish fear of humans in the remaining coyote population, which can resolve problems in both the short and long term. Other coyotes will move in to occupy vacant territory, so the removal of problem animals has no long-term negative impact on population numbers.

In a 2004 International Union for the Conservation of Nature status report on the conservation of wild canids (the scientific name for the family that includes coyote, dogs, and wolves), C. Sillero-Zubiri and D. Switzer wrote, "Realistically, in human-dominated landscapes where canids and people coexist there will only be, at best, an uneasy tolerance."

> *The coyote that saunters down a suburban residential street in broad daylight, ignoring the presence of humans, exhibits strikingly different behavior from a coyote that lives in the wild or a rural ranching community and survives because it has successfully avoided other predators, traps, snares, and gunshots.*
> *— Robert Schmidt and Robert Timm, "Bad Dogs: Why Do Coyotes and Other Canids Become Unruly?"*

TEACH THE KIDS!

Children should be taught how to recognize coyotes and instructed to keep their distance from the predators. Emphasize to children that they should never turn their backs and run from coyotes, but they should yell loudly for help while trying to climb up onto something, or get into a vehicle or building, to get away from a coyote that approaches them. The child should yell loudly but not shriek, since shrieking sounds are similar to that of wounded prey. If you see coyotes in your neighborhood, do not allow your children to play outside without adult supervision.

Additionally, Canadian authorities recommend teaching children the acronym BAM when faced with an aggressive coyote:

1. Back away

2. Act big

3. Make noise

Coyotes are found throughout North America, from residential subdivisions to industrial zones.

Avoiding
Coyote Conflicts

While conflicts with coyotes are occurring more regularly across North America, there are ways you can take action to avoid them. Coyotes are food opportunists, and it's this basic principle that brings coyotes into close contact with humans on a regular basis. Do not place food out for coyotes, or for any other wild mammals for that matter. Clean up under bird feeders, in the rows of vegetables in gardens, and under trees where seasonal fruits or berries may fall. Pet food or human garbage should not be left outside and made available for coyotes or other wild animals.

Small pets and their food can be major attractants for urban coyotes, and often pet owners have no idea that coyotes are in the area until a pet is seriously injured or killed. Keep cats and small dogs under close supervision during the day, but particularly at night. Some coyotes appear to seek out domestic cats as prey in residential areas, so consider keeping your cat inside at all times. Coyote-proof kennels or enclosures are another option to keep pets safe. Generally these enclosures should be at least 6 feet tall and have a wire apron around the bottom so that coyotes cannot dig their way underneath.

If you see someone intentionally placing food for coyotes, notify authorities. Although the offender may be well intended, providing coyotes with food provides an association of humans as a food resource. Managers at the Cape Cod National Seashore in Massachusetts threatened to close down beachside parking areas in Provincetown in November 2013 after nine coyotes were seen approaching parked cars in the area to beg for food. Apparently a number of people had decided to feed coyotes in that area, and the coyotes begin making a habit of approaching cars for food. People who feed coyotes are at risk of being bitten and have increased the risk of attack on their neighbors and others using the area.

Household trash should be placed in a container with a lid and placed outside the morning of pickup to provide less of an attractant to coyotes. Rinse trash cans with hot water and chlorine bleach on occasion to eliminate residual odors.

Installation of motion-detection lighting around your residence and outbuildings helps to deter coyote habituation. The use of game cameras with flashes has also been effective at repelling coyotes in some cases.

Crawl spaces under homes and outbuildings should be closed off so that coyotes cannot access these spaces. Clearing brush and dense vegetation on rural properties eliminates cover for coyotes and their prey. Wood and brush piles can attract small mammals, which then attract coyotes as well.

Avoid known or potential den sites and areas with thick vegetation where coyotes, and their prey, may seek cover. Never corner a wild animal; if you encounter a coyote, make sure it has an escape route to get away from you.

Coyotes are territorial mammals and conflicts with dogs can occur when a coyote attempts to assert dominance over disputed space—which can be a rural yard. Bold coyotes visit yards and howl and threaten larger dogs that they do not judge to be prey. Most of these incidents are territorial disputes, but a coyote may also see a dog as a potential mate.

When walking with your dog, keep the dog on a leash. If approached by a coyote, keep the dog under control and try to calmly leave the area, without running or turning your back on the coyote. If the dog is small, pick it up and carry it while yelling at the coyote and trying to appear big. Do not allow your dog to interact or "play" with a coyote. Do not get between a coyote and your pet, since the coyote may turn the focus of its attack to you. Never simply ignore, just watch, or turn your back on a coyote. Indifference can have the same effect as feeding a coyote.

Experts with Colorado Parks and Wildlife recommend that bold coyotes should be treated aggressively. Try to frighten the animal away by shouting and making loud noises. Make aggressive gestures such as waving your arms over your head to appear larger. Throw objects at the

Predatory attacks on humans can involve single coyotes or multiple animals in a pack.

animal, or spray it with a hose if one is available nearby. If you are in a group, stand together to appear larger. When you encounter a coyote, scan the area nearby to make sure the coyote is alone and that there is no danger from additional animals. Face the coyote, behave aggressively, and back away or move toward human activity or a building. If a coyote attacks you, fight back as aggressively as possible.

Bold coyote behavior should be reported to wildlife and public safety officials. Be aware that coyotes are often visible and active during daylight hours, so just seeing a coyote isn't reason for alarm. Coyotes are especially active from dusk through dawn.

If a coyote exhibits any sign of illness, such as acting lethargic, staggering, or appears to be having seizures, the animal may be rabid and poses a high risk to human health, so authorities should be contacted immediately. Other diseases affecting coyotes include mange, hepatitis, and distemper—all of which are contagious and can be transmitted either to humans or their pets

Timm and Baker and their research colleagues identified unusually bold behavior to include a coyote approaching people for food, attacking leashed animals that are accompanied by their owners, chasing joggers or bicyclists, and stalking small children. Coyotes exhibiting these behaviors pose an immediate risk to human safety and should be reported immediately to authorities.

Try to participate in recreational pursuits in the daylight hours. Take a walking stick with you on walks and hikes, and have a can of animal deterrent spray readily available. If you don't want to carry noise makers in a pocket or fanny pack, wear a whistle, and consider putting a few rocks in your pocket at the start of a hike so that you won't have to bend down to pick something up if you encounter a coyote. For some hikers, rocks-in-pockets becomes a routine at the start of every hike. Never discard food on a hike.

When camping, sleep inside a closed tent, and store food in coolers inside a vehicle.

Negative reinforcement is advised when dealing with coyotes, and it's a good idea to haze coyotes wherever you encounter them. Clap your hands, yell "Get! Go away!" or make other loud noises, and throw rocks or sticks—get the message across that coyotes are not welcome near humans. The loss of fear of humans is the bridge that takes a wild coyote into trouble with humans, so push back, for your safety and the welfare of the coyote. A coyote that bites a person must be destroyed.

Chapter 3
Gray Wolves

In summer 2009, thirty-two-year-old Candice Berner, a Pennsylvania native, moved to a remote Alaskan fishing village to work as a special education teacher. The school at Chignik Lake had about seventeen students at the time. Its mascot is a stuffed wolf that sits in a glass case in the lobby of the school.

"It's a great reminder of what lurks outside in the wilderness and to be on the alert at all times," Berner wrote of the wolf mascot in an October 2009 blog entry.

Berner was soon enjoying her outdoor adventures. As part of one of these adventures, she started a trap line with friends, and was hoping to trap a wolf because she wanted both the fur and the experience.

Berner loved the outdoors and was described by her dad as "small and mighty." Just under five feet tall, Berner liked to box (she participated in Golden Gloves boxing), lift weights (she was a powerlifter), and run (she ran marathons). She often took runs late in the afternoons, after school was dismissed for the day.

On March 8, 2010, Berner took off on an afternoon jog, following the road that connects the village to the nearby airstrip. She was never seen alive again. About 6 p.m., just a few hours after Berner had left on her run, four residents of Chignik Lake were returning to the village on snowmobiles and noticed some blood on the snow-covered road. The blood trail led to the brush where Berner's body had been dragged and fed upon by the wolves that killed her.

Investigators examining the tragic scene determined that the attack was predatory—the wolves had attacked and killed Berner as prey. Although she ran and fought the attack, the two or more wolves were much more powerful. Evidence in the snow indicated that one or two wolves chased Berner down the snowy road and attacked her, while a third wolf approached her from above the road, intercepting her effort at escape. Several wolves were located and killed in the area in the next few days.

The investigative report into the wolf attack on Berner stated, "This appears to have been an aggressive, predatory attack that was relatively short in duration." Genetic analysis of samples taken from the victim's clothing and from wolves killed near the attack site "positively identified one wolf and implicated others in the attack."

The report noted that, while wolf attacks on humans in North America are rare and poorly understood, "this investigation is the first where DNA evidence has been collected to confirm wolf involvement."

Investigators did not find any evidence indicating that wolves had become habituated to or had begun defending local food resources. They found no evidence that indicated biological factors, such as disease, predisposed the wolves to attack. The wolf confirmed to have been involved in the attack appeared healthy and in excellent physical condition.

The investigative report concluded: "In spite of the findings in this report, wolves are no more dangerous than they were prior to this incident, and people should not be unnecessarily fearful. However people should be mindful of the potential harm that wolves and other wild animals are capable of inflicting and always try to maintain a safe distance from wolves and other wild animals they encounter."

Aggressive Behaviors

The attack on Candice Berner was the second officially recorded human fatality due to wolves in North America in recent years, although numerous incidents of aggressive behavior and attacks have been recorded. In July 2006, a wolf attacked a twenty-five-year-old woman walking along an Alaskan highway. When the woman realized the wolf was approaching her, she ran. The wolf chased her down and bit her legs. The victim survived the attack after seeking shelter in a nearby campground outhouse.

In April 2000, a radio-collared wolf attacked a six-year-old boy in a logging camp in Alaska and attempted to carry and drag the boy into the forest. Adults rushed to the scene and were assisted by a dog in retrieving the boy from the wolf. According to a report written by Mark McNay and Philip Mooney in *The Canadian Field-Naturalist*: "The dog bit at the wolf's hind legs, but the wolf focused on the boy and largely ignored the harassment by both the dog and rescuers.... Eventually, when the dog positioned itself between the child and the wolf, a rescuer grabbed the boy and carried him away."

The boy in the Alaska attack survived with minor injuries, and the wolf was killed. McNay and Mooney noted: "Until the day of the attack, the collared wolf had never approached or acted aggressively toward people, but it had demonstrated increasingly fearless behavior. The habituation process was probably facilitated by the camp's central location in the small, isolated area of wolf habitat. The wolf probably encountered people frequently, but people would have been unaware of the wolf's presence during most encounters, because the camp, road, and sort yard were all surrounded by dense forest. The presence of dogs may have encouraged the wolf to periodically patrol and scent mark along the camp's perimeter. Company policy made it difficult for camp residents to hunt or trap near the camp or near worksites, thereby creating a de facto wolf protection zone where wolves were not conditioned to avoid humans. That pattern of frequent, low intensity (i.e., passive and inconsequential) encounters, irregularly spaced over a long period, is the ideal recipe for habituation."

Wildlife investigators concluded: "The animal's behavior during the attack clearly contained elements of predation. The wolf was killed shortly after the attack and found to be in normal physical condition; tests for rabies and canine distemper were negative. Low densities of ungulate prey and increased energetic demands associated with denning may have influenced the wolf's behavior, but we believe the wolf's habituation to people was a more significant factor contributing to the attack."

Carnegie Tragedy
Kenton Joel Carnegie wasn't as lucky when wolves attacked him in November 2005. The twenty-two-year-old engineering student

headed out for an afternoon walk in the woods around Points North Landing, a mining camp in Saskatchewan. In the week before Carnegie was killed, two other men encountered and beat back two aggressive wolves near the camp.

When Carnegie didn't reappear in camp at the time he was due, searchers headed out in the freshly falling snow and eventually found his partially eaten body. A pack of wolves had killed him. There was suspicion that the wolves had become habituated to humans after feeding at a nearby garbage dump.

Alaska wildlife biologist Mark McNay compiled information about wolf attacks in Alaska and Canada from 1970 to 2002, finding thirty-nine cases involving aggression toward humans among healthy wolves, with the infliction of numerous human injuries. These cases involved everything from wolves entering campsites and biting the human inhabitants to wolves entering camps to steal human clothing and other items. Some of these cases eventually escalated into attacks on humans. There have also been numerous attacks on pipeline workers in Alaska. In addition, McNay recorded three clear cases of predacious attacks on small children while the children were in the company of other people.

WOLF BITE

The biting pressure of a wolf's jaw is estimated at about 1,500 pounds per square inch (more than twice that of a large dog), according to the Minnesota-based International Wolf Center, allowing the animals to crush a moose femur in just a few bites.

Predatory Attack Trends

Mike Jimenez, Northern Rocky Mountain Wolf Management and Science Coordinator for the US Fish and Wildlife Service based in Jackson Hole, Wyoming, stressed in an interview that predatory attacks on humans by wolves are an extremely rare occurrence.

To paraphrase Jimenez, "If you look historically, there is lots of evidence of wolves attacking people, but if you put it in perspective, a wolf attack is really a rare event." He said, "I don't know of any scientist that thinks that wolves eat people as prey, other than in these rare instances."

Predatory attacks on humans usually involve a single wolf or a pack of wolves that appears to have learned that humans are prey.

Predatory attacks on humans usually involve a single wolf or a pack of wolves that appears to have learned that humans are prey. In these cases, victims are often directly attacked, often around the face and neck. In contrast to predatory attacks, a number of investigative attacks have been recorded in North America, in which wolves bite humans after approaching them closely in what is suspected to be testing behavior, or investigating the person as potential prey.

Five attacks on humans in Canada's Algonquin Provincial Park between 1987 and 2000 resulted in a new park policy to kill any wolves that show signs of fearlessness toward humans. The offending wolves in the Algonquin attacks had established "regular patterns of fearless behavior" for weeks before the attacks.

Although the number of wolf attacks on humans in North America may not seem high, wolf attacks around the world have much higher human mortalities. Researchers, led by John Linnell of the Norwegian Institute for Nature Research, conducted a detailed review of wolf attacks, concluding with publication in 2002 of the paper "The Fear of Wolves: A Review of Wolf Attacks on Humans." They found reports of wolf attacks resulting in the deaths of 440 people in northern Italy from the fifteenth to the nineteenth centuries. None of the wolves involved had rabies. Linnell's report noted that sixty-seven people, including fifty-eight children, had been killed by wolves in one Italian valley between 1801 and 1825. Similar attacks occur in other areas, with non-rabid wolves killing more than 200 children in the Hazaribagh region of India between 1980 and 1995, according to Linnell. This region has a long history of wolves killing humans.

The differences between wolf attacks in North America and in other regions of the world may be explained by differences in how humans treat wolves. Traditionally, humans have persecuted wolves in North America, but in many other regions of the world, wolf hunting has been restricted.

American wolf biologist Steven Fritts noted: "How wolves react to humans depends on their experience with people. Wolves with little negative experience with people, or wolves that are positively conditioned by feeding . . . may exhibit little fear of humans."

Linnell and his research team also noted that wolves "have been so heavily persecuted during the last century that it is highly likely that there has been intense selection against 'fearless' wolves or those that are not very shy of humans. In countries where wolves are hunted (legally and illegally) it is unlikely that any will live long once they begin to develop 'fearless' behavior."

American wildlife managers have recognized that wolves can become habituated to humans and human activities just as readily as bears or mountain lions, but also assert that wolves may not require a consistent pattern of food conditioning before attacks occur.

The common thread in all North American wolf attacks involving human injury seems to be a loss of fear of humans—habituation as the result of nonconsequential encounters. One biologist noted that the transition from nonaggressive behavior to aggressive attacks on humans can be rapid and unpredictable.

"Wolves are these animals that wander, checking their home range out constantly, trotting, probing to see what's available," Jimenez said. "Wolves are very curious too, so a lot of times they are always checking things, but it's not to seek you out as prey. But they are very, very curious and that presents problems.

"Predation is a whole series of steps and behaviors. It's not that you go out and kill something. You spend time searching, looking, finally seeing something, running and chasing it down, catching it, subduing it, killing it, and finally eating it."

The attack sequence Jimenez describes refers to wolves hunting game animals like elk as prey, but what about humans?

"The difference is, with elk, deer, and livestock, that is a clear potential prey base. What you see, research-wise, and from historical data, [is that] people are not. There are rare instances where people have been a prey base . . .

"When [wolves] see an elk, they see a potential food source, so they go through this series of behaviors. When they see people, there may be curiosity, there may be habitation, but there is not [the instinct that says] 'this is a potential food source.' There are rare instances when that has been the case, and when that does happen you clearly see it, and it's [targeted at] kids. It's children, and it's women."

The reason for the focus on women and children is because, in most cases, they are the most vulnerable. In certain places around the world, such as parts of India, where there is not a lot of natural prey, poor children in rural villages become targets as a prey base.

A 1999 Royal Swedish Academy of Sciences report detailed the long-standing problem of "child-lifting" by wolves in India, in which packs of wolves hide in the vicinity of a village during the day, with most attacks involving one wolf grabbing a child in the evening as the children play outside, and retreating into the forest where the

The common thread in all North American wolf attacks involving human injury seems to be loss of fear of humans.

pack feeds upon the victim. Five wolf packs preyed on children in sixty-three villages, with eighty casualties in two years (1993–1995), and only twenty victims were rescued. Most of the children were three to eleven years old. As appalling as this report is, wolf attacks are not unusual in India and some other places in the world.

Back in North America, the need to take aggressive action to prevent human habituation of wolves has been recognized by Yellowstone National Park officials. The reintroduction of gray wolves to the park in the mid-1990s resulted in an expanding wolf population that is very visible to thousands of park visitors each year. The park's policy for management of habituated wolves notes that habituation appears to be a prerequisite for an aggressive act toward a human. But the second key factor is humans who act in a nonaggressive manner, which may influence (or "invite") aggressive canine behavior. Park managers work to educate the public about how human behavior can lead to habituation by wolves, and also conduct hazing and aversive conditioning on wolves to discourage the animals from engaging in close encounters with humans.

Wolves such as those in Yellowstone National Park have the potential to come into fairly close contact with human activities, so park managers monitor the situation closely, recognizing that a high degree of tolerance toward humans may be acceptable, but certain behaviors are not. These unacceptable behaviors include:

- approaching people without signs of fear
- entering human developments without fear
- becoming habituated to humans and human food
- acquiring human foods at least once
- attacking or injuring a human

In accordance with National Park Service policy, if a wolf doesn't respond to hazing or aversive conditioning, or has particularly aggressive behavior, it will be removed from the population, usually by killing, to keep the animal from injuring a person.

Wolves become habituated to humans as readily as other predators but may not receive food rewards before attacks on humans occur.

AVERSIVE CONDITIONING

Hazing and aversive conditioning are recommended to discourage wolves from becoming habituated to humans.

Aversive conditioning techniques against wolves vary, but all are designed with the goal of giving the predator a negative association in attempt to eliminate undesirable behavior. For example, in certain situations, Yellowstone National Park officials may fire nonlethal munitions (cracker shells, beanbags, or rubber bullets) at wolves when they come into campgrounds or approach humans so the wolves have a negative experience when approaching human-occupied areas.

It is not definitive that aversive conditioning techniques change wolf behavior other than at a specific locality. For instance, if wolves approach a campground occupied by people and are met by rangers shooting rubber bullets at them, the wolves may leave, but the lesson may only apply to that locality. The wolves may approach people in other areas, but may avoid the specific location where the negative experience occurred.

"Chasing [wolves] out of sheep does not make them not go after sheep," Mike Jimenez of the US Fish and Wildlife Service notes. Instead, the wolves may seek out a sheep herd that is not as well protected, or where no negative consequence has been experienced.

"It does change the behavior at the locality, but to say that wolves won't approach people again because they got blasted at one place, I'd say that data is sketchy," Jimenez says. "They are very smart, and they are very good at exploiting a situation to their advantage."

An investigative attack is one in which wolves bite a human after approaching closely in what is suspected to be testing behavior, or investigation of the person as potential prey.

In Yellowstone National Park, where public hunting is not an option, federal officials have killed habituated wolves on several recent occasions. In May 2009, a yearling male wolf was frequently seen in close proximity to humans in developed areas of the park, including around Old Faithful. The wolf's undesirable behavior escalated, as the animal repeatedly chased people on bicycles and motorcycles. The wolf began approaching people and vehicles and behaved as though it expected to receive food rewards from humans. When hazing failed to change the animal's behavior, the wolf was determined to be a threat to human safety and was killed by federal wildlife officials.

Federal officials also killed a habituated wolf in Yellowstone National Park in October 2011. Over several months, the 110-pound male wolf had approached park staff and visitors at close range at least seven times, according to a press release from the agency. Repeated attempts to haze the wolf away from developed areas of the park failed, and after ripping apart a ranger's pack in search of food, the wolf was killed. The wolf's history of fearless behavior in the presence of humans, and its obvious food-conditioned behavior, led to its eventual demise.

Park service officials insist that sightings of wolves in close proximity to humans and developed areas indicate that a dangerous situation could be developing and should be immediately reported. Yellowstone park officials maintain strict sanitation policies within the park to prevent any of the park's wild predators from becoming food conditioned, a situation that poses a clear danger to human visitors.

More Northern Attacks

In July 2012, parks officials in Canada shot and killed a wolf that had stalked a man walking with a small child and a puppy in a park. The family was walking through an established campground in Kananaskis Country (west of Calgary) when they noticed the wolf was following them. The family escaped into a nearby restroom, but the wolf waited outside for some time before eventually wandering away. Park officials had received numerous reports of this wolf in the week preceding this incident, as it approached vehicles, lunged at a passing motorcyclist, and chased bicyclists. The wolf was highly habituated to humans and had likely become food conditioned as well.

In December 2012, a wolf attacked an Alaskan trapper on his snowmobile, biting the man. According to the *Fairbanks Daily News-Miner*, the thirty-year-old man was snowmobiling down a frozen creek with his father when the single black wolf attacked, grabbing the man's arm. The trapper fought back, and man and wolf tumbled hard onto the ice, with the man on top. The wolf yelped and began to retreat. When it stopped to look back, the trapper yelled at the animal and it proceeded to leave. The man underwent a series of rabies vaccinations. Because the attack took place in a remote area, in extremely cold temperatures, state wildlife officials were unable to recover the animal for rabies testing.

LEARNED BEHAVIOR

The offspring of wolves raised near humans transmit human-habituated behaviors to their offspring.

Dick Thiel of the Wisconsin Department of Natural Resources makes a good case that the development and spread of human-habituated wolves can be traced to learned behavior passed from one wolf generation to the next. Thiel developed a list of behavioral indications associated with certain wolf packs in Wisconsin, including:

1. wolves refusing to move out of the way of oncoming vehicles

2. wolves laying in the open on roads and roadways

3. wolves walking through or bedding down in residential areas

(next page)

4. wolves establishing rendezvous sites within regular visual range of humans

5. wolves approaching occupied vehicles

6. wolves approaching people on foot

Thiel documented that the offspring of litters of wolf pups raised near humans transmit habituation behaviors to their offspring.

Frequent inconsequential encounters with humans can lead to habituation.

In March 2013, it was reported that a Manitoba woman drove herself to the hospital after being attacked by a wolf near Grand Rapids (north of Winnepeg). The woman said she had stopped along the road to see if another motorist needed help, and the unprovoked attack occurred while she was outside her vehicle. The woman received injuries to her neck, and the wolf reportedly followed her back to her vehicle. She received treatment for her wounds and underwent rabies shots. A witness to the attack claims that he saw the woman offer the animal food before the attack, but whether this claim is true remains unknown.

In August 2013, a sixteen-year-old boy was injured in a wolf attack while sleeping outside his tent in an established campground near the shore of Lake Winnibigoshish in north-central Minnesota. The Minnesota Department of Natural Resources reported the boy sustained multiple puncture wounds and a laceration about 11 centimeters long to his head. The wolf ran into the woods after the boy kicked it, and the boy was transported for medical treatment for his injuries, which were not life threatening. The US Forest Service campground was evacuated, and other campers interviewed by investigators reported numerous incidents involving the wolf biting through tents and otherwise failing to exhibit a fear of humans. Federal animal damage control officials trapped and killed the wolf a few days later. The adult male wolf weighed about 75 pounds and was found to have a deformed jaw and other abnormalities. State wildlife officials speculated that the animal's deformities could account for its lingering in the campground, where it could search out easy food sources, and eventually became habituated to humans, with the resulting dangerous behavior.

In October 2013, a forestry worker in British Columbia was confronted by a pack of wolves as she walked back to her truck with two dogs. The pack came within 10 feet of the woman, and as she reached for her bear spray, one of the dogs began fighting with the wolves. The woman was unharmed, escaping to safety in the truck with the other dog. The dog that battled the wolves was severely injured and had to be euthanized. The British Columbia Forest Safety Council issued a safety alert, advising forestry workers in the area about how to react in such situations, including taking defensive action.

Bikes and Motorcycles Attract Attacks

In June 2013, a motorcyclist testing a new bike in Kootenay National Park, Alberta, nearly hit a wolf in the roadway, but swerved to avoid the animal. The man turned around and approached that area of the highway with his camera in hand, only to have the wolf jump back onto the highway and begin chasing the bike. The wolf crossed a line of traffic to pursue the motorcycle, and the motorcyclist was able to snap pictures of the animal in hot pursuit, ears flattened against its head, running at full speed. The bike eventually outran the animal, and the motorcyclist appeared to have enjoyed the encounter, likening the wolf to his pet dog, which liked to chase bikes. Wildlife managers at Parks Canada took a different view, noting that the animal appeared to be habituated, causing concern for wildlife managers. In the coming days, the wolf was seen repeatedly along the same stretch of highway, and it appeared that the wolf had been receiving food rewards from passing motorists.

In July 2013, a bicyclist had a harrowing encounter with a wolf while cycling on the Alaska Highway. Mac Hollan, thirty-five, of Idaho, was on a long-distance ride to raise money for a school lunch program when he found himself far ahead of his partners and suddenly being chased by a wolf, with the animal lunging at his foot. Hollan pedaled for his life, repeatedly squirting the wolf with blasts from the can of pepper spray he'd stashed in his handlebar bag. But the wolf kept returning to chase and attack, ripping the bike's panniers, spilling tent poles onto the highway, and ripping the tent.

In his first-person account posted on Facebook, Hollan expressed his fears of what would happen next as he approached an incline on his bike.

"I just kept thinking about all the shows I have seen where wolves simply run their prey until they tire and just finish them," Hollan wrote. "It was a surreal moment to realize that I was that prey, and this hill was that moment."

Fortunately an RV came around the corner, and its driver quickly assessed the scene and stopped to help save Hollan from the wolf. Hollan was able to get inside the vehicle while the wolf attacked the bike he'd jumped off. The wolf continued its attack on the bike while numerous cars arrived on the scene, with people yelling and throwing rocks and vehicle horns honking. Eventually someone hit the wolf in the head with a metal water bottle, and the wolf retreated to the side of the road. The bike team was able to recover the bike and proceed on their trip thanks to the help of fellow travelers, who didn't leave until the men had safely pedaled away.

Wolves typically test things to see if it's potential prey. So when something runs away, there's an instinctual response in the wolf to go after it. "With something like bikes and cars, it's a mixed signal inside," the US Fish and Wildlife Service's Jimenez said. "Something tells [the wolf] to chase it, get it, but what are you going to do with a 5,000-pound truck when you catch it? But that doesn't click."

Because it's so instinctual for the wolf to chase, most scientists recommend that if you have an encounter with one (or any big predator), do not run.

"You are trying not to trigger that response, where the animal gets hyped up and triggers the chase," Jimenez said. "That's upped that behavior to the next step. It's not just inquisitive, now you've got the animal in full-bore chase [mode]. It's a little harder for a wolf to turn the whole sequence of events off."

Protection and Habituation

Residents of areas occupied by expanding wolf populations in the United States have reported bold behavior from wolves, which were granted protection from persecution in the early 1970s with their listing under the Endangered Species Act. Wolf biologist Steve Fritts and his coauthors wrote, "The apparent increase in aggressive encounters after 1970 was thought to be the result of greater protection for wolves and increased wolf numbers, combined with increased visitor use of parks and other remote areas."

Jimenez agrees, and views habituation due to protection as a problem: "If you look at what kind of thing leads to problems with predators—and wolves are no exception—habituation is a big one. When animals start getting used to being around people, then you start seeing a pretty predictable pattern."

That pattern involves wolves coming closer and closer as they encounter people but don't experience negative consequences. They become bolder in their actions, which includes being seen in human-occupied areas in broad daylight. Wolves are top-of-the-food-chain predators, and they tend to assert their presence. When they approach human-occupied areas, the wolves enter cautiously, but when not met with a negative consequence, they come closer. When faced with something big, like a human, the wolves either view the presence as a threat and retreat in response, or they exert dominance.

Providing food rewards when wolves go near human-occupied areas not only diminishes any negative consequence, but actually provides the wolf with a positive reward for its efforts.

Human habituation is one of the main causes of conflicts between wolves and humans.

"Protected areas are a real breeding ground for habituation," Jimenez said. "Protected status—having wolves listed as endangered—definitely contributes to habituation. The way you manage them, even the way you list them if it equates to protection, changes the way the wolves respond to people. There is no negative reinforcement [that] says that people are bad news—that heads [wolves] down that habituation path."

Habituated wolves are often destroyed by wildlife managers because of the threat the animals pose to human safety.

"It's a predictable and sad ending, but when wolves lose their wildness, [that's] what happens," Jimenez said.

The Impact of Hunting Wolves

The recent delisting of wolves in some areas of the Northern Rockies and in the Great Lakes area, and the initiation of hunting seasons in those areas, may prove to be important for management by reinforcing fear behavior in the wolf population and eliminating those animals that appear to have lost fear and thus may pose a threat to human safety.

John Linnell and the group of Norwegian scientists who reviewed wolf attacks on humans recommend that wildlife managers do what they can to keep wolves wild and out of trouble with humans. They also recommend that any wolves that appear to have lost their fear of humans or act in an aggressive manner be removed from the population. These researchers note, "Carefully regulated hunting may be useful in maintaining shyness in some situations, and will, in addition, provide a feeling of local empowerment and control over the wolf situation."

Jimenez said his view is that hunting is a positive thing for wolves because it can influence behavior. He said: "If you have wolves that become easy around people, easy around houses, easy around ranches, those are probably not real suitable habitat for wolves. Having people have the legal ability to hunt them, to harvest them, is a selection process that says the ones that are smart stay in more remote areas, where we'd like to see predators hang out. Those are the ones that survive and pass on their traits to their offspring.

"Animals definitely learn," Jimenez said. "So hunting, on a behavioral level, will definitely change wolf behavior."

Jimenez predicted that after a few years of state-managed hunting seasons, people wouldn't see wolves in hunted areas, walking along the roads, or approaching people. "Wolves, in areas where they are exploited for hunting or for livestock control, are much more leery of people than wolves that are protected," he said.

Habituation Harms Wolves

Yellowstone National Park officials know that wolves within the park are habituated to humans, and when they wander out of the park during hunting season, the wolves are vulnerable. Numerous wolves that inhabit the park during a portion of the year have been killed in legal harvest in adjacent states.

"Wolves that are comfortable around people don't last long during hunting seasons," Jimenez pointed out. "It's the consequence of having wolves be used to people."

But the reality is that the regulated hunting of wolves does not hurt stable wolf populations.

And predators that have lost their fear of humans pose a special danger. Predatory attacks by wolves on humans may be rare events, but that is no reason to discount the risk of such an attack. People don't need

Nonaggressive behavior toward wolves can invite an aggressive response.

Most cases of aggressive wolf behavior occur in areas where wolves are free from persecution.

to fear wolves, but they do need to be cautious, and to realize that if a wolf appears to be at ease around people, it may pose a risk to human safety. The wolf itself may be in jeopardy because of this behavior.

Jimenez urges, "Don't habituate wolves, because somebody else is going to have to deal with them."

> *Most of the recent cases of wolf aggression occurred where wolves were protected, such as national, state, or provincial parks, or near large industrial sites located in remote wilderness areas (mines, oilfields, logging camps).*
> *—Alaska Department of Fish and Game: (2008) Wolf Safety in Alaska*

Avoiding
Wolf Conflicts

People who live and recreate in areas that are inhabited by wolves need to consider safety. Try to avoid behaviors that would encourage wolves to spend time near people and near areas of human development.

Keep children and pets close and under supervision, especially if there are daytime sightings of wolves in your area. While hiking, do so in groups, with children in the middle. Children should never be left unattended in an area known to be occupied by wolves.

Keep a clean camp, with garbage secured and food stored in animal-proof containers. Don't cook food or wash dishes near your sleeping area. Do not leave pet food outdoors, and keep dogs on a leash and at your side. Never leave a dog unsupervised and tethered at a campsite or cabin. And, as hard as it may be, do not try to save a dog from a fight with a wolf.

The Wisconsin Department of Natural Resources cautions that hunters using camouflage, special scents, and calls may find themselves in an encounter with a wolf that has failed to recognize that the hunter is a human. If approached by a wolf under such circumstances, make your presence known by standing, shouting, or throwing objects at the animal.

Use motion-detection outside lights to deter wild predators from using areas around your home. Eliminate habitat for wolf prey species from your residential yard, and discourage the feeding of wild animals, such as deer, which can attract wolves and other large predators.

Carry bear pepper spray, and have it accessible, while recreating in wolf country, and know how to use it (see page 31 in the "Black Bears" chapter for a refresher on how to use spray).

If you see a wolf, there's a fairly good chance that it's habituated, meaning that the wolf is used to being around people (or else you wouldn't be seeing it). Habituated wolves can associate humans with food, which means the wolf poses a risk to human safety. When you see a wolf, realize that you are viewing an animal that can kill animals more than ten times its size—this is a formidable predator.

Reacting to Wolf Encounters

If you encounter a wolf, stay calm and don't run. A frightened or nervous wolf will hold its tail between its legs. A wolf that runs away, while stopping for a quick look back every now and then, is not a threat. Do what you can to reinforce to the animal that humans should be avoided.

Respond aggressively to a bold wolf, standing your ground and fighting back. Never run from a wolf.

A wolf exhibiting defensive behavior may dash toward you at a run, veer away, and bark. If a wolf barks at you in an encounter, it's alarmed. The animal could have a den site or animal carcass nearby, so slowly back away. Never turn your back on the wolf. If you are suddenly surrounded by a pack of barking wolves, you are almost certainly at a den or rendezvous site, and you need to deliberately retreat.

Sometimes wolves will watch and "test" you. The animal may move around you, approaching at a slow walk, or even bounding forward. It may try to grab your shirt or jacket sleeve as it continues its testing behavior, and it may seem friendly or playful. This requires aggressive action on your part. A wolf that is conducting testing actions is a wolf that is testing your suitability as prey. Stand tall—wave your arms around overhead to try to appear larger. Be loud. Yell and throw rocks or other objects at the wolf.

A wolf with hackles up and holding its tail high is showing aggression. You should demonstrate some aggression on your end in response to this.

A wolf with its ears flattened and its lips back in a snarl is warning of an imminent attack. Aggressively fight back. If you are in imminent danger, do whatever is necessary to protect yourself.

If you encounter an aggressive wolf, again, stand tall and try to appear large. Yell, clap your hands, throw objects, lunge toward the animal—be aggressive in your actions. Keep your eyes on the wolf and don't bend down or turn your back to the animal. Stand your ground and fight. Use noisemakers, firearms, bear spray, walking sticks—anything you can grab as a weapon. Retreat to safety if you can do so without turning your back on the animal. Escape into a vehicle, a building, or even up a tree.

Be sure to alert other recreationalists and wildlife authorities about your encounter with an aggressive wolf, so that action can be taken to lower the risk to others.

CONFLICTS INVOLVING DOGS

Domestic dogs and wild wolves are involved in dozens of conflicts each year. Under various circumstances, wolves may view dogs as competitors or challengers for territory or food, as potential breeding partners, or as prey.

Small dogs are often viewed as prey, which wolves easily and frequently kill and eat. Some wolves learn that residential areas harbor dogs, which the wolves then turn to as a food source. Do not leave pets outside overnight unless in a sturdy kennel, and do not release dogs outside after dark in areas where wolves are present.

If hiking in wolf country with your dog, keep the dog leashed and close to your side. If you are in an area where there is concentrated wolf use, reconsider your use of the area. Wolves have been known to approach people hiking with leashed dogs and to kill the dogs, in apparent disregard of the presence of humans, especially from May through July, when wolves may be defending a den or rendezvous site. If you do hike with a dog, make noise as you move, so the wolves will hear that a human is present. Placing bells on the dog's collar may also reduce the likelihood of an encounter. Keep an eye out for wolf signs (tracks, scat, animal bones, etc.).

Hunting hounds are at risk when hunting in wolf territory. The baying of hounds may be viewed as a territorial challenge to wolves, which then quickly move in and kill the hounds as they pursue game. The high-risk time period for hunters using hounds appears to be July through September, when wolf packs are tending to pups at rendezvous sites. December also poses a higher risk, as the winter breeding season approaches.

Consult with your local wildlife officials about the presence of wolves in your area, and about the best way to keep your dogs safe while hunting. The best way may be simply to avoid areas with concentrated wolf use.

Chapter 4

Mountain Lions

It was January 8, 2004, in Orange County, California. Mark Reynolds had stopped his mountain bike on a trail in Whiting Ranch Wilderness Park—more than 4,000 glorious acres of oak woodlands, canyons, and rolling hills, with steep slopes covered in coastal sage scrub and chaparral. Reynolds was an avid cyclist, even, on occasion, hitting up fellow riders for donations to help provide bicycles to kids whose families couldn't afford them. Reynolds was bent at the waist trying to put a broken chain back on the bike when the mountain lion hit him. The attack left thirty-five-year-old Reynolds dead. The lion then dragged the man's body into the brush. After consuming part of his victim's body, the lion partially covered the remains before turning back to the trail for his next victim.

Anne Hjelle, a thirty-year-old former Marine, was enjoying a bike ride with a friend when the lion sprang from the brush alongside the trail and landed on Hjelle's back. Knocking her to the ground, the lion grabbed Hjelle's head in its mouth and began dragging her off the trail and into the brush. But her friend, Debi Nicholls, wasn't far behind, and Nicholls wasn't going to give Hjelle up without a fight. Nicholls grabbed hold of one of Hjelle's legs and began a tug-of-war with the lion in an attempt to save her friend, screaming all the while. Two other cyclists had found Mark Reynolds's disabled bike along the trail when they heard the screams of a woman nearby. Discarding the bike, the men ran to help Nicholls in her fight to save Hjelle and were able to pelt the lion with numerous rocks, convincing the lion to release its hold and move away into the brush.

Hjelle survived the brutal mauling, and the resulting 200 stitches and five operations that were part of her recovery. She has written a book about her recovery and is now an inspirational speaker. The mountain lion that attacked Hjelle—a 122-pound adult male in good condition—later returned to the attack site and was shot and killed by wildlife officials. It was only after the investigation began on the attack on Hjelle that the body of Mark Reynolds was discovered, where the big cat had cached it off the trail near the disabled bike.

Most mountain lion attacks on humans are predatory in nature, and the best response is always to fight back.

The killing or hunting of mountain lions is illegal in California, and has been for years. These large predators have little reason to fear humans, and this lion had begun to treat humans as prey. It's a pattern that is repeated across the countryside.

Ten years after the fatal attack in Whiting Ranch Wilderness Park, on a sunny day on the last weekend in March 2014, Madison Smith and her two children were walking on a trail in the park when Smith saw a mountain lion racing forward from the brush, fixated on her five-year-old son. Another hiker arrived and helped to scare the animal away by yelling and brandishing a tree branch, placing himself between the small children and the predator. But the lion was persistent, approaching the group repeatedly—at times just a few feet away. A passing group of mountain bikers stopped to help, and the larger group—numbering about twenty-five people by the time the ordeal was over—was able to chase the lion back into the brush. When deputies and wardens arrived on the scene, the yearling male mountain lion began to approach the group and was shot and killed. This well-used trail is located near an elementary school.

Adult mountain lions are large, powerful predators at the top of the food chain, weighing in at 85 to 120 pounds for females, and 120 to 180 pounds for males. They can be as long as 8 feet from nose tip to tail tip. Preying mainly on deer and elk, mountain lions also hunt and kill a variety of small prey, including rabbits, mice, birds, and domestic pets and livestock.

The California Department of Fish and Wildlife receives hundreds of reports and complaints about mountain lions every year. And every year, between three and a dozen mountain lions are determined to pose an imminent threat to human safety and are subsequently killed in that state.

Increased Risk of Attack

In 1991, after a series of lion attacks on humans in California, Texas, and Colorado, wildlife ecology professor Paul Beier took on the task of tallying the number of verified mountain lion attacks on humans in the United States and Canada, discovering nine attacks involving ten human fatalities, and at least forty-four nonfatal attacks, from 1890 to 1990. Beier reported there were more fatal attacks in the later twenty years than in the previous eighty years.

Most of the victims documented in the Beier study were children, and these children were with other people when the attacks took place. Researchers learned that even captive mountain lions show a heightened interest in children.

Beier found that not all of the attacks took place in the great outdoors; in some cases, mountain lions came into buildings after their victims. In one case, a mountain lion crashed through a window after a person. In another case, a lion came into a Colorado garage to attack a small child.

Mountain lion attacks on humans in California have increased in recent years, with nine attacks in that state from 1985 to 1995. Researchers have discovered a pattern of lion behavior that indicates attacks may be imminent. There is an increased risk of attack on humans when these things happen:

- High mountain lion populations are located close to urban areas.
- An increase in lion sightings occurs.
- Lions demonstrate little or no fear of humans.
- Lions attack pets.
- Other patterns of close encounters with humans are noted.

Lee Fitzhugh of the University of California, Davis, points out that prey recognition is a learned behavior in cats. For example, one mountain lion could learn from another mountain lion that a strange animal is prey if the two are together at the time of a successful attack. In addition, mountain lions could be stimulated to attack if the strange animal (such as a human) behaves in a way similar to the lion's normal prey species. Such behavior includes running and quick movements.

> *[Mountain lions] have evolved over thousands of years to hunt for prey that moves on four legs. They go after prey that represents the greatest opportunity for the least amount of risk.*
> —*Colorado Parks and Wildlife*

Since learned behavior can influence prey selection, mountain lions can learn to select humans and their pets as a food source. Again focusing on learned behavior, mountain lions can learn to avoid areas where they are harassed.

Female mountain lions are more prone to attack than males.

An increased pattern of mountain lion sightings or close encounters between humans and lions is cause for concern, according to Fitzhugh, and "should elicit management action to prevent an attack."

The public must be warned that close encounters with mountain lions are extremely dangerous. "Warnings should be direct and severe. Mountain lions are no animal to consider lightly, and people should be told forcefully that lions are dangerous," Fitzhugh wrote in a paper presented at a mountain lion management workshop. "We must inform the public that mountain lions can be dangerous to people. There seems to be a public impression that they are not."

That impression is one that requires continued attention. When mountain lions were spotted roaming in Santa Barbara, California, in 2012, the *Santa Barbara Independent* ran a column titled "Talking to the Mountain Lion." It was written by Laura Stinchfield, a self-proclaimed pet psychic and animal communicator, or as she says, "I can telepathically talk to animals."

Her June 1, 2012, column noted that a mountain lion had been hanging around a nearby school, and she talked to that mountain lion. The lion proclaimed it was in the area to eat bunnies, adding, "I do not prey on people." The conversation concluded with this piece from the lion: "It's getting harder to live in peace with humans close, and your species is harming the environment. A natural state is becoming hard to achieve. I'm sorry that people cannot read my body language. I am no harm to them. Humans seem to have no eye for balance. All other animals can read my intentions."

Behavioral Patterns

The Oregon Department of Fish and Wildlife (ODFW) 2006 Oregon Cougar Management Plan lists specific "behavior pattern criteria" that prompt agency concern for human safety. When practical, ODFW will attempt to remove offending cougars if one or more of the criteria are met. According to the plan, all animals contacted under these circumstances will be humanely euthanized.

When a lion turns the "fur" side of its ears forward like this, holding its head low to the ground, its body language indicates an attack is imminent.

The plan's behavior pattern criteria include:

- Aggressive actions directed toward a person or persons, including but not limited to charging, false charging, growling, teeth popping, and snarling

- Breaking into, or attempting to break into, a residence
- Attacking a pet or domestic animal
- Loss of wariness of humans, displayed through repeated sightings of the animal during the day near a permanent structure, permanent corral, or mobile dwelling used by humans at an agricultural, timber-management, ranching, or construction site.

Where a cougar is causing damage, being a public nuisance, or posing a public health risk, and ODFW personnel or its agents are called to respond, the animal will be humanely euthanized. Under no circumstances will consideration be given to relocation of cougars.

The plan explains: "All opportunities to explain and educate the public about the rationale behind lethal removal shall be utilized. These include not only the potential for future danger, but also cougar population biology (particularly territoriality and intra-specific competition and mortality), legal liability, and our policy of not moving a potential problem animal to another location where someone else's pets, livestock, or family could be put at risk."

Lion expert Lee Fitzhugh recommends that, once a lion has attacked a person, the animal has exhibited behavior that recognizes humans as prey, and that animal must be removed from the population.

"Even though removal may not eliminate the possibility of another attack, failure to do so almost certainly will increase the probability of another attack because of learned predator identification behavior," Fitzhugh said.

LION BEHAVIOR

There are several elements of mountain lion behavior outlined by lion expert Lee Fitzhugh and predator control specialist David Fjelline that are relevant to how humans should react when encountering the animals:

1. Most mountain lion attacks on humans are predatory in nature. Fighting back is the best response. In no cases has "playing dead" been effective at ending an attack.

2. Mountain lions are threatened and intimidated by large, strange objects approaching rapidly and from above. Thus, appearing larger is advised. Positions above the cat are positions of dominance, and positions below the cat are subordinate.

3. Mountain lions are stimulated to attack by small objects that move rapidly across or away from their line of travel. Do not run, and fight back in a physical encounter to disrupt the animal's prey drive. Throwing an object at the cat can provide enough disruption to end the encounter.

Aggressive behavior from humans encountering mountain lions lessens the odds of the situation progressing to an attack.

Attacks across the Continent

Of the more than forty mountain lion attacks on humans in North America cited by Daryll Herbert and Dan Lay in a 1997 paper titled "Cougar–Human Interactions in British Columbia," about half occurred in British Columbia, and, more specifically, on Vancouver Island. It is likely that hunting of mountain lions has helped to significantly reduce interactions between mountain lions and people, but restrictive mountain lion hunting regulations, combined with increasing mountain lion populations and increases in prey populations, have resulted in an increase in attacks on humans in these areas. In addition, many areas and parks set aside for human recreational use around the country restrict or prohibit hunting.

There have been numerous attacks over the years involving mountain lions pouncing on adult humans, and they occur across the country and in a variety of situations. In 2001, a thirty-year-old ballet dancer was killed while cross-country skiing in Banff National Park. The mountain lion had hidden behind a tree, and when the woman passed by, the lion leapt upon her back, killing her. A wildlife warden killed the large male mountain lion as it fed on her body. This appeared to be a predatory attack—but it was one of three incidents involving at least two different mountain lions in the Banff area that day. Earlier that morning, a pet dog was mauled by a mountain lion while in its backyard, but the pet owner was able to scare the lion away and the pet survived the attack. A few hours later, another woman walking her dog was stalked by a mountain lion. A neighbor heard her screams for help and opened his door to the woman, allowing her to escape. Officials expressed confidence that the mountain lion involved in the pet attack, and in the stalking of the second woman, was not the same animal that killed the woman earlier in the day. Banff National Park is closed to the hunting of wild predators (or other animals), and wildlife is accustomed to human presence. Prey species such as elk move into residential areas to graze, and the wild predators follow.

While out for a run in a state recreational area east of Sacramento, California, in April 1994, forty-year-old Barbara Schoener was attacked and killed by a female mountain lion. Evidence indicated the lion attacked the woman from a ledge, and that she fought back before being killed. The female lion fed on her body and buried it in debris before bringing her cub to the site to feed again. About a week after Schoener's remains were discovered, the female mountain lion was killed just feet from the attack site, and her cub was captured and placed in a zoo.

In December 1994, a 130-pound male mountain lion killed fifty-eight-year-old high school teacher and bird-watcher Iris Kenna in California's Cuyamaca Rancho State Park, about 50 miles from San Diego. It appeared the woman had survived the initial attack, but the cat caught her from behind and killed her. The lion was shot in the area the same day. This state park has a history of conflicts between mountain lions and people. In 1993, the year prior to Iris Kenna's fatal encounter, a mountain lion chased two horseback riders, and later attacked a girl and her dog. The lion was later shot and killed.

In one of the more disturbing attack stories, in August 1996, thirty-six-year-old Cindy Parolin was killed in a mountain lion attack in British Columbia. Parolin and three of her children were horseback riding when a lion rushed out toward the horses. It attacked six-year-old Steven when he was thrown from his horse. Cindy Parolin jumped from her horse to fight off the lion, ordering her two other children to get Steven to the safety of their car and to get help. The woman survived her battle with the mountain lion for more than an hour, even as the lion fed on her body, only succumbing to her injuries after learning that her children were safe. The lion was shot and killed at the scene. Steven Parolin survived his injuries.

In 2008, a fifty-five-year-old autistic man was killed and eaten by a mountain lion near his New Mexico home. An aggressive mountain lion was later shot in the man's yard, but escaped. The adult male lion was eventually caught and killed.

Colorado's Front Range contains not only the state's largest cities and a majority of the population, but is also a hot spot for human conflicts with mountain lions. Residents and recreationists enjoying the outdoors are brought into conflict in this urban interface, where hunting is restricted or prohibited. In June 1990, twenty-eight-year-old medical student Linda Walters was jogging near Boulder, Colorado, when she encountered not one but two mountain lions. Although she threw objects and yelled at the cats, they approached her and she retreated up a nearby tree. One of the lions started up the tree after her, so Walters kicked it, knocking it from the tree. The second lion tried to get to Walters, but she smacked it with a tree branch and it retreated to the ground as well. The lions waited nearly half an hour under the tree but finally turned their attention elsewhere, which is when Walters made her escape.

In January 1991, eighteen-year-old Scott Lancaster was attacked and killed by a mountain lion as he jogged near his Colorado high school. The 100-pound adult male lion, which had fed on his body and partially covered it up with debris, was shot at the attack site by law enforcement officers investigating Lancaster's death.

In August 2012, wildlife officials in Boulder were forced to shoot one young adult mountain lion and scare off a second after the duo were seen wandering around the city, showing no fear of humans while inspecting residential areas and yards.

Four months later, a thirty-year old woman was hiking off the trail with her dog near the Sunrise Amphitheater in Boulder when she spotted a mountain lion just a few feet away. The woman raised her hands and made noise, making her way to the safety of an outhouse nearby, where she and her dog hid out while the lion sniffed around outside for several minutes before departing.

Just a few days later, and 100 miles south, people using Cheyenne Mountain State Park in Colorado Springs, Colorado, started having their own troublesome encounters with a mountain lion. One female jogger was chased by the animal; park rangers heard the woman's screams and ran over to save her from possible attack. Although lion tracks were found in the area, the animal was not found.

In January 2013, state officials had to remove a young male lion from the city of Lyons, Colorado, after it was seen preying on animals within the city. First the lion killed a raccoon near a residence, and when a domestic cat came out to inspect, it killed the cat too. All too aware of the pattern of escalating behavior, officials decided to remove the animal to protect the public.

Around this time, neighboring states were getting in on the action. Three mountain lions (an adult female and her adolescent cubs) were euthanized in Utah by state officials after preying on pets in a residential area of Woodland. Things were more harrowing in California in February 2013. David Nash was stalked by a mountain lion while hiking on a trail at dusk near Colfax, in the foothills of the Sierra Nevada. When the lion blocked his path on the Stevens Trail and would not retreat, Nash was able to use his cell phone to call for help. Officers from the California Highway Patrol were dispatched in a helicopter to assist and discovered Nash waving a flashlight with the big cat standing nearby. The pilot used the helicopter to fly in low and drive the lion away, and then hovered over Nash with a bright spotlight until he met up with other officers on the trail. A spokesperson for the California Department of Fish and Wildlife noted, "The behavior was consistent with a mountain lion that is stalking prey." The next morning, a state wildlife officer went to the trail to post warning signs, only to be confronted by the aggressive lion. As the lion prepared to pounce, the warden shot and killed the animal.

Young mountain lions may get into trouble when preying on pets in residential areas.

USING PEPPER SPRAY ON MOUNTAIN LIONS

Since mountain lions, wolves, and bears (both black bears and grizzly bears) inhabit some of the same areas, carrying and knowing how to use bear spray (pepper spray) is a great idea to help deter an aggressive encounter with a large predator.

In 2001, a mountain lion biologist with Montana Fish, Wildlife & Parks successfully used bear spray to deter an adult female lion that had approached two researchers and their lion hound, which was held on a short leash. The lion approached the men within just a few feet and had attempted to slap the dog with a paw when she was sprayed in the face. The lion turned away, but quickly returned to resume the attack, only to be met with a second burst of spray. The lion retreated about 20 yards distant and laid down, foaming at the mouth. This gave the men, and the dog, time to retreat from the area. Wildlife officials have since changed their research protocol to no longer directly approach radio-collared females with tiny kittens, as was the case in this encounter.

Pepper spray must be carried in a way that is accessible in an emergency, and be of sufficient size that you can get several bursts of spray from it if needed. Each burst should last two or three seconds.

In addition to humans, pets and other animals were not immune to attacks from mountain lions. Because researchers believe that these attacks may be a precursor to attacks on humans, the predator is destroyed. A pair of mountain lions stalked a residential district in British Columbia in February 2013, targeting family pets, until conservation officers killed one of the cats. A hunter killed the second lion the next day. Both animals were two years old and in great physical condition. The predators had learned that the residential area provided easy prey in the form of family dogs that were let out into their yards. The big cats were seemingly indifferent toward the presence of humans, hunting pets near homes and despite outside lights and disturbances. Officials estimate there were ten attacks on pets within a period of a few weeks before the lions were killed.

In a story repeated in numerous states each year, sharpshooters are deployed into residential areas to destroy mountain lions that have followed their main prey source (deer) into neighborhoods. The big cats are discovered through close encounters with homeowners who find lions eating fresh deer kills on their lawns, or when they let their pets outside only to have mountain lions quickly dispatch their pets as prey. Sometimes the pets are snatched from the leashes of their owners while they walk—and when lions become this bold, most wildlife officials will take aggressive action to kill the cat to protect human safety.

For example, in December 2013, officers in Canmore, Canada, killed two mountain lions in a residential area after the predators killed several pets. Canmore is located in a wildlife-rich area just outside the entrance to Banff National Park. One of the mountain lions was killed on an outside deck at a residence. The second lion was killed when the officer walked back to a dog that had been killed by the lions; it refused to retreat as the officer approached. The site was only yards from an incident that occurred three days prior, in which another dog had been attacked and killed while being walked on a leash. Tracks indicated that the woman and her dog had unknowingly been followed for some time prior to the attack. Although wildlife officials expressed concern that such bold mountain lions could proceed from killing dogs to attacking their human companions, there was still criticism of the actions taken to protect the public.

In other cases, a person may be injured in the process of trying to protect their pet. In early 2013, a Washington state woman was knocked down and scratched by a mountain lion after the woman tried to save her dog from the attacking predator. The woman had just let her small dog out into the yard in a well-developed residential area in the middle of the night when the lion attacked her pet. A sheriff's deputy arrived at the scene not long afterward and killed the lion in the woman's yard.

Mountain lions don't just attack in wooded areas or in large backyards. Some get a little too close to human dwellings. A Manitou Springs, Colorado, man looked out the picture window of his mountain home in March 2013 and found an adult mountain lion peering through the pane. As the man investigated further from within the confines of his residence, he found three other mountain lions inspecting his home. Wildlife managers fear that wild predators demonstrating a lack of fear of humans and human-inhabited areas pose an increased risk to human safety, and some go so far as to state that an animal's loss of wariness indicates that the risk of attack on humans has increased.

British Columbia conservation officers shot and killed two mountain lions in March 2013—one of the animals was just steps away from a daycare facility. The young male mountain lion was in poor condition, and was seen in a tree near where children were playing during recess. The daycare supervisor spotted the animal, hurried the children inside, and called for help. Once wildlife officials determined the cat was in poor condition, it was destroyed. The other cat was destroyed after it entered a barn and killed the livestock harbored inside.

In May 2013, an off-duty park ranger was attacked by a mountain lion as he fished on the beach in Redwood National and State Parks in California. The man saw his dog being chased by a mountain lion. As the lion approached, he yelled and the lion changed its focus to attacking the man. He fought the animal, hitting the attacking lion several times with his fishing pole and kicking it several times until it retreated. The subadult mountain lion was killed in its nearby hiding place later that day.

South Dakota officials promptly reacted to an emerging pattern of dangerous behavior by mountain lions in the small Black Hills town of Keystone in early May 2013. An adult female lion and her two 40-pound cubs were killed after the lion family spent two weeks demonstrating their presence in a very visible way on town streets, threatening pets, strolling through yards, and even killing a deer on a street near the post office. State wildlife officials killed a fourth lion that same week in the Angostura Recreation Area after finding the lion lingering near a recreational trail, watching people as they hiked and biked. A park ranger observed the lion for nearly half an hour as it intently watched people from a distance of about 20 yards. The state's regional wildlife supervisor said the cat's lingering in the area, and its bold behavior, led to the decision to kill the animal because of the threat it posed to the unsuspecting public.

Hunting Controversy

Delwin Benson of Colorado State University notes that the historic pursuit and persecution of mountain lions by humans and dogs has helped to reinforce the cat's secretive and elusive behavior, thus encouraging their desire to keep their distance from humans. Mountain lions that encounter humans with no negative consequences learn to tolerate people, and their desire to retreat is dulled. Benson suggests mountain lions should be subject to "aversive behavioral conditioning," such as being pursued with hounds until the lion flees, to reinforce the lesson that humans are threats and should be avoided. Lions would thereby learn that humans are not intruders, and neither are they a prey species.

Voters in some states have banned the sport of hunting mountain lions with hounds in an attempt to protect the big predators, and others have banned lion hunting almost entirely. Wildlife managers believe that when heavy localized hunting results in the harvest of older mature males, more young mountain lions are likely to disperse into these areas, creating an increase in conflicts because young cats are more likely to be involved in close encounters with humans. Wildlife managers in Washington were slated to begin putting this theory to the test in 2013 with the implementation of a new mountain lion management plan. The plan is based on "equilibrium management," in which hunters will remove no more than the surplus of animals that would be generated through natural reproduction, estimated to be 14 percent of each management area's lion population.

A study by researchers associated with the Large Carnivore Conservation Lab of Washington State University concluded: "Heavy harvest corresponded with increased immigration, reduced kitten survival, reduced female population growth, and a younger overall age structure. Light harvest corresponded with increased emigration, higher kitten survival, increased female population growth, and an older overall age structure."

A 2013 paper on mountain lions in western Washington in the *Journal of Mammalogy*, written by Brian Kertson of the University of Washington and colleagues, recommended that natural resource agencies focus on management strategies targeting problem individuals and maintaining old-age structures in local mountain lion populations, combined with proactive landscape planning and public education in residential areas, to reduce conflicts between humans and their wild feline neighbors.

DEFENSE WITH A FIREARM

Although there has been speculation that even if a person is carrying a weapon when attacked by a predator, the victim won't have the time or ability to use it correctly, this has been disproven when it comes to victims of attacks by mountain lions. Researchers report that most people who had a firearm when attacked used the weapon effectively, typically killing the mountain lion and ending the encounter.

Walter Howard of the University of California, Davis, has advocated that mountain lions must be hunted to be managed properly, noting that mountain lions are normally shy and wary predators not commonly seen by hikers, hunters, or other people. When mountain lions become very visible, and begin to turn their prey drive toward pets and domesticated animals, Howard maintains these are clues that the lion population has grown too large. He suggests that to show true compassion for lions, wildlife agencies should use licensed hunters as predators to maintain healthy populations of lions in suitable habitat.

Oregon's 2006 mountain lion management plan seeks to maintain the state's mountain lion population "at a level well above that required for long-term sustainability." At the same time, it seeks to resolve conflicts, noting "specific areas with elevated conflict may also be targeted to reduce conflict by reducing cougar numbers." These targeted areas thus serve as buffer zones of low cougar density to reduce conflicts.

While Oregon's human population increased 24 percent from 1990 to 2003, the mountain lion population also increased; the estimated population is more than 5,000 animals. Although mountain lions are a hunted game species in Oregon, a 1994 ballot measure banned cougar hunters from using dogs. In early 2013, a number of eastern Oregon counties considered the possibility of opting out of the statewide ban. Legislation was proposed that would give county governments the ability to exempt themselves from the law if local voters approved such a measure, but the bill was quickly defeated.

Most western states allow the public to hunt mountain lions with hounds (with the exception of California, Oregon, and Washington). Using hounds allows hunters to tree the cats and have a good look before taking a shot. This discrimination allows hunters to walk away from lactating females and select for adult males if desired. The Wyoming Game & Fish Department reports that 90 percent of mountain lions harvested by hunters in that state are taken with the use of hounds.

In addition, laws allowing the use of hounds to hunt mountain lions have spawned a new industry of treeing lions for photography—a practice sportswriter Douglas Chadwick called the "big predator equivalent of catch-and-release fishing." Researchers wanting to place radio collars on mountain lions to study lion ecology also use hounds to tree the animals so they can be sedated and worked on.

Assessing Risk

The most recent assessment of factors governing the human risk of mountain lion attacks was undertaken by the US Geological Survey's David Mattson and colleagues, as published in the spring 2011 issue of the journal *Human–Wildlife Interactions*. Their review indicates that the number of confirmed physical attacks on humans by mountain lions increased by four- to fivefold between the 1970s and 1990s, but has stabilized at around four to six attacks per year since 2000.

If a lion is spotted at a distance and appears to be directing its attention away from people, it is exhibiting indifference. Such an animal poses only a slight risk to humans.

Some of the important management findings of the Mattson study:

- Young mountain lions in poor condition are more likely to threaten people.
- Adult mountain lions are more likely to cause death when they attack.
- Possession and use of firearms is effective at preventing physical contact while in a close encounter with a mountain lion.
- Mountain lion attacks, and deaths from attacks, are more likely if children are present during a close encounter.
- Adult intervention reduces the chances that an attacked child will die from a mountain lion attack.
- Aggressive behavior from humans in close encounters with mountain lions lessens the odds of attack.
- The presence of dogs during the day reduces the odds of a mountain lion attacking a person.

Researcher Paul Beier of the University of California noted that there is no such thing as "zero risk" when it comes to mountain lion attacks on humans, but there is ample support for removal of offending animals when attacks occur. He concluded, from the cases he reviewed, that "when an attacking cougar was not removed, there was a 30 percent chance of a second attack within 50 miles and two years. . . . Thus it appears that leaving the offending animal in the wild may increase the risk of a future attack."

Continued Conflicts

Local governments and agencies continue to struggle with public perceptions of mountain lion ecology and management. In 2013, public reaction to the killing of several problem mountain lions in California—where lions are listed as a "specially protected species" under a state law that makes it illegal to hunt, harm, capture, or harass them with the exception of certain circumstances—prompted

Adult mountain lions are more likely than juveniles to kill the victim.

wildlife officials to adopt new rules expanding the use of nonlethal methods to address problem cats.

On average, fewer than 3 percent of California's reported mountain lion encounters resulted in the animal being identified as an imminent threat to public safety and subsequently killed. In 2009, there were 141 incidents between mountain lions and humans reported in California, and one lion was killed to protect public safety. In 2010, there were 127 incidents, with seven lions killed. In 2011, there was an increase to 214 incidents, but only three lions were killed. In 2012, 162 incidents were reported, and seven lions were killed.

But the December 2012 killing of two starving mountain lion kittens in Half Moon Bay, California, sparked outrage among animal activists. The juvenile lions were frequenting residential areas, and efforts to haze them away from the area failed. The animals were finally found hiding under a deck during a rainstorm, and game wardens shot and killed the pair. Only after the animals were killed was it revealed the starving kittens weighed about 13 pounds each.

The California Department of Fish and Wildlife issued an internal agency bulletin detailing the agency's policies on human–mountain lion interactions in March 2013, noting: "Recent incidents have resulted in multiple mountain lions being taken in a single depredation or public safety event. Historically, such events are rare. These cases have concerned the Department and the public and have prompted the Department to review policies and procedures regarding how the Department responds to all mountain lion interactions."

The bulletin noted: "The Department's foremost consideration is the protection of human life. Responding to public safety wildlife incidents are a priority for the Department and a public safety mountain lion shall be humanely euthanized as quickly as possible by a Department official or a public safety peace officer."

A lion spotted at a distance, sitting in a position facing away from human activity and showing little interest in humans, poses little threat to human safety.

The killing of the two kittens prompted California state senator Jerry Hill to introduce Senate Bill 132, requiring state wildlife officials to use nonlethal options when dealing with mountain lion incidents where there is no imminent threat to human life. The bill easily passed the California Assembly, and in September 2013, California governor Jerry Brown signed the new mountain lion protection bill into law. Senate Bill 132 amends the state's law to read:

> (a) Unless authorized in this chapter, nonlethal procedures shall be used when removing or taking any mountain lion that has not been designated as an imminent threat to public health or safety.
>
> (b) For purposes of this chapter, "imminent threat to public health or safety" means a situation where a mountain lion exhibits one or more aggressive behaviors directed toward a person that is not reasonably believed to be due to the presence of responders.
>
> (c) For purposes of this chapter, "nonlethal procedures" means procedures that may include, but are not limited to, capturing, pursuing, anesthetizing, temporarily possessing, temporarily injuring, marking, attaching to or surgically implanting monitoring or recognition devices, providing veterinary care, transporting, hazing, rehabilitating, releasing, or taking no action.
>
> (d) The department may, as the department determines is necessary to protect mountain lions or the public, authorize qualified individuals, educational institutions, governmental agencies, or nongovernmental organizations to implement nonlethal procedures on a mountain lion in accordance with subdivision (a).

Animal advocates hailed the legislation as a landmark in lion conservation, while reporters noted that the law prevents game wardens from killing lions that venture into populated areas of the state unless the animals pose an urgent threat to human safety. Early indications are that California wildlife officials will have ample opportunity to test the new legislation, and the public's reaction, as human encounters with mountain lions continue. A mountain lion was documented via surveillance camera as it roamed the streets of the Hollywood Hills in early 2014. In February 2014, a fifty-year-old homeless man was treated for extensive injuries from a presumed mountain lion attack at his encampment near Perris (about 70 miles from downtown Los Angeles).

Mountain lions are powerful predators at the top of the food chain.

Outside of California, conflicts also continue. Officials in Saskatchewan issued cougar advisories in March 2013 after lions were spotted near two different elementary schools. Citizens were cautioned to keep watch on their small children and pets while outside, since cougars are known to attack smaller people.

Chino Valley, Arizona, officials had to deal with two mountain lions after about twenty residents of a neighborhood gathered outside to watch the lions as they explored the area in April 2013. The adult female and her yearling offspring spent most of a day in the neighborhood, under the watchful eye of wildlife officials, until they could be herded out of the area by wildlife managers in their vehicles.

In September 2013, a sixty-year-old woman was severely injured by a mountain lion while gardening near her home on Flores Island, off the west coast of Vancouver Island, British Columbia. The mountain lion jumped the woman from behind, and the woman's husband fought the animal off using a spear. The animal was wounded and fled, but was found dead nearby by wildlife officials investigating the attack. Conservation officers were familiar with the scene, as the woman had reported several run-ins with a lion two months prior, but weather conditions hindered the search for the animal at that time. Newspaper accounts noted that the couple kept a boar spear handy in case of problems, and that they had lived in the area for more than three decades.

Just a few weeks after the garden attack, another mountain lion was reported to be harassing area residents. Incident reports include a mountain lion ripping out a screen door while attempting to gain entry to a home, and an account of a mountain lion stalking a person. These dangerous behaviors are indicative of a pattern of increased risk of attacks of humans.

In early October 2013, a bicyclist on a popular Jackson Hole, Wyoming, trail came around a corner and was confronted by a mountain lion at a close distance. The man attempted to scare the animal away by raising the bike over his head and yelling, according to the *Jackson Hole News & Guide*, but the animal reacted with a predatory stalk. The man used pepper spray, which deterred the cat enough that the bicyclist was able to escape the scene.

Avoiding
Mountain Lion Conflicts

So why is it that attacks have been on the rise? Well, there are simply more mountain lions and more people using the same habitat, so increases in conflicts are to be expected. For example, Montana officials note that more than 70 percent of lion–human interactions in that state involve one- to two-year-old animals establishing their own territories. That's a pattern that other states have reported as well.

Colorado State University's Benson suggests that prevention of mountain lion attacks on humans could involve the following components:

1. Reducing the density of mountain lions through sport hunting

2. Limiting human use of mountain lion habitat (either temporarily avoiding problem areas, or through permanent zoning and use restrictions)

3. Modifying existing habitat to limit availability of prey

4. Conditioning humans to avoid lion encounters

5. Aversive behavioral conditioning of lions to instill fear/avoidance behavior

Fitzhugh and colleagues updated Beier's earlier tally of fatal and nonfatal mountain lion attacks on humans and reviewed the circumstances of these attacks and how victims responded. Lessons learned from this exercise include:

- Gunshots were less effective at deterring an attack than yelling or screaming. Gunshots were only effective when the lion was actually shot and killed. Only a few lions left the area as a result of shots being fired to scare the animals. Researchers suggest that if a gun is to be fired to frighten a lion (instead of shooting to kill it), it should be repeatedly fired in quick succession.

- In some cases, a human lunging at a mountain lion has actually managed to scare the animal away. There were several cases in which humans charged at the lion, and in some cases scuffled with the animal, before the animal fled the scene.

- Solitary hikers are three times as likely to be attacked by a mountain lion as those who travel in pairs or larger groups.

- Sleeping out in the open (outside of a tent or building) has resulted in numerous attacks by lions, but most involved minor injuries when the victim woke up and fought back. In most cases, it appears the cat was simply dragging away moribund prey, only to be startled away when the victim awakens and makes noise. Such an incident occurred near Nevada City, California, in July 2012, as a camper slept in his sleeping bag next to the Yuba River. Around 1 a.m., the sixty-three-year-old man awoke to a mountain lion biting his head and clawing at him in the bag. The man protested and the cat retreated. The man received medical treatment for his injuries.

Homeowners should be aware that planting vegetation desired by deer draws not just deer to residential neighborhoods, but the mountain lions that prey on them. Trim brush and reduce landscaping that provides cover for mountain lions, and deer-proof your yard by not landscaping with plants that deer like to eat. Install outdoor lighting or motion-sensitive lighting around your home to discourage predator presence. Don't feed wildlife, or leave pet food outside for predators to find. Keep pets secure.

When enjoying the outdoors, take action to reduce the likelihood of encountering a mountain lion. Try to recreate in groups, and be aware of your surroundings, scanning areas nearby as you move around. Be aware of the presence of animal carcasses—often revealed by the odor and presence of magpies and ravens. A mountain lion feeding on a kill or defending a food cache can be very dangerous. It's a good idea to carry a walking stick—it could become a defensive weapon in an encounter with a lion. Make noise, and do not wear earphones. Do not run at dawn or dusk, or alone. Keep children in the middle of your group, and always within arm's reach.

What to Do If You Encounter a Lion

If you encounter a mountain lion, you may be in danger and need to react accordingly. First and foremost, stay calm and try to assess the situation. Each lion is an individual and you must take your cues from the animal. The Washington Department of Fish & Wildlife recommends:

- Keep the lion in view at all times. Stay upright and facing the animal.

- Without bending over, pick up small children and hold them in your arms.

- Speak calmly but firmly. Be assertive in relaying that you are not prey.

- Moving slowly, back away. Do not turn your back, and do not run. Make sure the lion has an escape route.

- Try to appear larger—raise your arms, open your jacket. If you are in a group, stand shoulder to shoulder to appear bigger.

Understanding Predatory Lion Behavior

Researchers Fitzhugh and Fjelline developed a list of predatory mountain lion behaviors, along with suggested appropriate human responses:

If a lion is less than 50 yards away and intent toward a human, it may be curious, but still poses a risk to human safety.

- If the lion stares intently, follows and hides, or hisses, snarls, or vocalizes, you are in substantial danger of attack.
- If the cat approaches you, throw rocks and other objects, but don't crouch down. Yell loudly.

- If the cat crouches, with its tail twitching, ears erect, and body low to the ground, get ready to fight because an attack is imminent. If you are carrying pepper spray, or have a firearm ready, take careful aim and use it!

A mountain lion hiding and intently staring is assessing the success of an attack, posing a substantial risk to human safety.

- If the cat's ears are turned so the fur side is forward, and if its tail is twitching and its hind feet are pumping in preparation to jump, you are seconds away from physical combat. Attack the mountain lion aggressively, such as by running at the animal with a stick, trying to gouge the animal's face.

- If the mountain lion attacks you or another person, fight back aggressively. Try to stay on your feet and fight, fight, fight with every means possible!

Never "play dead" in a lion attack. Assert aggression at any lion you encounter.

HAZING SENDS A MESSAGE

Negative conditioning techniques are used to haze mountain lions away from populated areas, such as shooting individual lions with beanbags or rubber buckshot. "It sends a strong message to reinforce the cat's natural instinct to avoid people," according to Colorado Parks and Wildlife.

Mountain lions can learn to select humans and their pets as a prey source.

Even when accompanied by adults, children are targeted for attack by mountain lions.

FOR KIDS ONLY

Since kids, due to their smaller size, are often viewed as prey by mountain lions, it is important that you teach children how to react if they see a mountain lion. Colorado officials suggest using the acronym SMART to help children remember what to do:

S: Stop. Do not move right away. Do not run.
M: Make yourself as big as possible, such as by raising your arms over your head.
A: Announce yourself. Talk loudly to the animal.
R: Retreat. Back away slowly.
T: Tell an adult.

Chapter 5
Grizzly Nightmares

On one hot August night in 1967, two nineteen-year-old women—in separate incidents—were killed by two separate grizzly bears in Montana's Glacier National Park. While camping with her boyfriend under the stars, Julie Helgeson was dragged from her sleeping bag and severely mauled by a grizzly. When the search party found her a few hours later, Helgeson was still alive. She was carried to the nearby Granite Park Chalet where a surgeon (a guest staying at the lodge) tried to save her, but she had suffered major blood loss. A priest prayed with the young woman as she died.

Less than a dozen miles away, another grizzly bear raided a campground occupied by a group of five young people. While the others escaped by climbing trees, Michele Koons was caught in her sleeping bag and was dragged off into the dark by the grizzly bear. Her body was recovered the next morning.

Glacier National Park rangers had an obligation to find and destroy the offending bears to protect the public from further tragedy. Rangers stationed themselves on the porch of the chalet for the next few days, shooting grizzly bears as they approached to feed in a nearby garbage dump, which had allowed visitors to watch the bears feed from the relative safety of the deck. Rangers killed three grizzlies, including the sow responsible for killing Julie Helgeson, as well as the bear's two cubs.

Two rangers stationed near Trout Lake, where Michele Koons was killed, were sent to investigate the mauling the next morning. Three days after recovering Koons's body, two rangers shot and killed a sow grizzly near the attack site. It was soon confirmed this was the grizzly that had killed Koons. A cleanup crew later hauled out loads of garbage that had accumulated from years of sloppy camping at the site.

In both cases on that tragic night in Glacier National Park, the camping parties were sleeping out in the open, not in tents. Both bears had fed on garbage, associated humans with food, and had lost their fear of humans. One of the bears had demonstrated aggression to humans in the days prior to the fatal attack, and those familiar with it wanted the animal destroyed, but the National Park Service was slow to act. Bear attack expert Stephen Herrero called the bear "predisposed" to attack in his book *Bear Attacks: Their Causes and Avoidance.* He wrote: "It was an aggressive individual encouraged to be so by the outcomes of its many interactions with people and their garbage and food. . . . [T]his bear's long experience in getting food and garbage from people led it to decide to treat a person as prey."

Herrero added: "The odors and activities of people were well known to each bear. When the opportunity presented itself in the form of unsheltered campers, each bear acted like a predator."

At the time of the Glacier attacks, bears were still feeding from open garbage dumps in other parks, including Yellowstone National Park. But the fatal attacks in Glacier had wide impacts. Yellowstone officials decided it was time to shut the dumps down, removing a significant food source for the park's bruins. Although long-time grizzly bear researchers Frank and John Craighead had advised that the dumps be phased out over a longer period of time, and that a monitoring program be established to track the movement of the bears and supplemental food (such as elk carcasses) be provided during the period of adjustment, their recommendations were not followed. Some feared that abruptly shutting off an important food source for bears could result in more human injuries, not less.

"The deaths in Glacier had generated considerable pressure to avoid similar incidents in Yellowstone at all costs, "explained Frank Craighead in his 1979 book, *Track of the Grizzly.* "Yet conditions at Yellowstone were quite different. The grizzlies had been using the Yellowstone dumps as a source of easily obtained supplemental food for eighty years, but food foraged from the dumps was not associated directly with man, as were the handouts they received at Glacier."

The park service began reducing the amount of garbage available to bears in both Glacier and Yellowstone parks, and abrupt dump closures occurred in Yellowstone in 1970 and 1971. Bears were getting into campgrounds and causing conflicts throughout

Yellowstone; subsequently, they were removed, killed, or relocated continually. There were eighty-eight grizzly bear deaths in the Yellowstone region in a two-year period (including deaths by agency action, natural causes, and illegal kills).

In some cases, bear managers trap and relocate grizzly bears that approach human developments too closely.

On August 23, 1970, Yellowstone park visitors found a human scalp on a blanket. Evidence was collected from the scene and stored. On September 16, 1970, rangers found an abandoned camp that had been ransacked by a bear. Cans of food had been mouthed by the bear but unopened, indicating the bear might have been old and toothless. Rangers removed the camp but the occupant was never found. A month later, and less than a mile away, an old, partially toothless sow grizzly was trapped and ear-tagged after hanging around a developed area of the park. Her new ear tag identified her as bear 1792. She was relocated to an area about 18 miles distant in an attempt to keep her out of the developed area.

Did the human scalp found less than a month prior originate in the ransacked camp? Had the camper been the victim of a bear mauling? Was bear 1792 responsible? No one will ever know, but suspicions about the incident remained for years. This 1970 death was unpublicized until another death brought the case to light.

In 1971—the year when the last park dump was closed—there were no injuries or deaths from bears in Yellowstone—the first time in fifteen years. The record was soon broken, with a human mortality the next year.

In June 1972, twenty-five-year-old Harry Walker was killed by a grizzly bear as he walked with a friend back to his illegal campsite in the Old Faithful Geyser area at around midnight. An old, mostly toothless sow grizzly was trapped and killed at the campsite the next day—bear 1792. Bear 1792 was identified as Harry Walker's killer, but in reality, was Walker her second victim?

National Park Tragedies Continue

Four years after the bear 1792 incidents in Yellowstone, tragedy struck at Glacier National Park once again. In September 1976, Mary Pat Mahoney, who was part of a party of campers, was dragged from her tent, killed, and partially consumed by an adult male grizzly bear. Less than two hours later, two young male grizzlies that had recently been involved in numerous cases of aggressive behavior toward humans, as well as consuming human food and garbage, were destroyed by park officials. Human blood was associated with one of the bears, implicating at least one of the duo in Mahoney's death.

The park deaths kept happening—1980, in particular, was a deadly year for grizzly encounters. A teenage couple was attacked while sleeping outside their tent one July night in Glacier National Park. Both were killed and partially consumed. They had camped a half mile from a small garbage dump that was located on land outside the park's jurisdiction. The bear responsible for the fatalities was shot and killed nearby.

A month later in Banff National Park, three people were mauled by the same bear in separate, surprise-encounter attacks. Two had severe injuries but survived, while one man, Ernest Cohoe, died a few days later in a hospital. The adult male grizzly bear responsible for the attacks weighed more than 700 pounds. This was an aggressive bear with a history of feeding on human garbage. The attacks occurred because of the dangerous combination of a human-habituated, aggressive bear coming into close contact with humans.

BEAR HIBERNATION

Bear hibernation may last up to seven months. During hibernation, bears may not eat, drink, urinate, or defecate. They may lose 24–43 percent of their body weight during hibernation.

Young grizzly bears like this one are ideal candidates for aversive conditioning—teaching the animal to maintain a distance from humans.

The same month as the attacks in Banff, Glacier was the scene of yet another fatality. A thirty-three-year-old man was killed and partially consumed while camping alone. Few details are known, but an adult male grizzly known to have shown aggression toward people was soon destroyed, and evidence linked him to the fatal attack.

Yellowstone Sees More Trouble

After a few years of relief, the mid-eighties brought a resurgence in attacks and fatalities in Yellowstone National Park. These attacks were horrendous and predatory in nature, and inflicted by grizzly bears attacking during the night. In the summer of 1983, one of two men sleeping inside a tent was dragged outside and substantially devoured by a grizzly bear. The adult male grizzly that killed the man was soon trapped and killed nearby. This bear was well known to researchers as being habituated to humans, but not aggressive.

> *Grizzly bears entering camp at night and methodically starting to chew on people, in contrast to grizzlies who charge and attack, are most likely acting as predators.*
> —*Stephen Herrero,*
> Bear Attacks: Their Causes and Avoidance

The next summer, twenty-five-year-old Brigitta Fredenhagen of Switzerland obtained a backcountry permit for the Astringent Creek Trail in Yellowstone National Park. Fredenhagen set up a tidy camp adjacent to the hiking trail and stashed her food away from the camp, suspended between two trees. She was sleeping alone when she was pulled from her tent and killed by a grizzly bear during the night. The bear partially consumed her body. The bear responsible for her death was never found.

Every one of these bear attacks on humans took place in areas where grizzlies were granted fully protected status—in and around national parks throughout the Northern Rockies. The bears had no reason to fear humans and, in many cases, had become accustomed to human presence. Yet rather than viewing humans as benign, the bears turned to them as prey. Things would be quiet in the parks of the Rocky Mountains for a number of years, until another fatal attack occurred in 2005 in Canada.

Pushing for Changes

In June 2005, thirty-six-year-old Isabelle Dube was jogging with two of her friends on a hiking trail near a golf course at Canmore, Alberta (near the southeast boundary of Banff National Park), when they came around a bend and spotted an adult male grizzly bear on the trail in front of them. Dube decided to climb a tree, but her two jogging partners backed away and ran to the golf course clubhouse for help. The 200-pound bear pulled Dube down from the tree and killed her. When a wildlife officer arrived on the site, he shot and killed the bear.

Signs warn outdoor enthusiasts to be prepared to avoid a bear attack.

This bear had been relocated from the area just a few weeks prior, after it had made repeated visits to the golf course and had approached a woman walking a small dog. Still, wildlife officers denied that the bear had exhibited aggressive behavior and claimed they had moved the bear simply to discourage it from approaching populated areas.

In his 2007 book, *The Politically Incorrect Guide to Hunting*, Frank Miniter wrote of his belief that Dube's death was avoidable: "After all, if grizzly hunting had been allowed in the area, certainly any bear brazen enough to approach people would have been shot quickly." Miniter also suggested his belief that, at the very least, biologists should have used aversive conditioning to reinstill a fear of humans into the bear.

Under certain conditions, National Park Service officials will initiate programs of hazing and aversive conditioning to correct inappropriate behavior of grizzly bears rather than remove the animals from the population due to conflicts. According to Yellowstone's bear management plan, "Early intervention may prevent bears from becoming conditioned, thus minimizing the need for relocation or removal, minimizing the risk of accidental or illegal mortality, and minimizing the risk of human injury."

The hazing techniques can vary—from using sirens, horns, cracker shells, or "bear bangers/screamers" to the use of trained bear dogs to harass bears away from developed areas or areas of human use. Other techniques include shooting bears with nonlethal rubber bullets or other "thumper" devices, as well as capsicum spray.

In addition to reducing the rate of bear-caused human injury and property damage, aversive conditioning (defined as a specialized form of learning imposed upon an animal to punish it for behavior that is deemed undesirable) helps to establish a fear of humans in bears that might otherwise become dangerous due to their habituation to humans. Ideal candidates for aversive conditioning are often young bears (yearlings to subadults) when they first encounter humans or situations involving a potential food reward. Adult bears that have repeatedly received food rewards and have lost their fear of humans are not good candidates. Wildlife managers decide on the use of these techniques on a case-by-case basis.

In 2009, Glacier National Park officials were faced with the need to remove a grizzly bear family from the population due to the danger it posed to the public. The incident reports involving this adult female grizzly and two litters of her offspring dated back a decade, but the first incidents of concern were recorded in 2004, when park managers received reports of a female and her two cubs approaching campers. The reports indicate the bears were "comfortable near humans and would not defer to humans." Reports in 2004 and 2005 indicated the bear family was unresponsive to groups of people when they tried to scare the bears away from campsites and food preparation areas in developed portions of the park. The reports came in: a bear sniffing a tent zipper in the middle of the night; a horse party of six people being approached by a sow bear at very close range.

These behaviors led federal park managers to initiate a program of intensive aversive conditioning aimed at the bear family. The program was apparently successful, as reports from the 2006 season indicated that the bears displayed either desired or neutral behavior when encountering humans.

But in July 2009, the reports started to come in again: the bear family approaching campsites, sniffing tents, and not showing any deference to human presence. In one case, the sow behaved in an irritated manner, while her cubs were curious and unafraid as they explored an occupied campsite. When rangers began to intensively monitor this family group, they found the sow "purposely approaching" rangers, even after the rangers had given up ground to the bear.

According to the findings of a National Park Service board of review, "Managers deemed the group to be conditioned to humans and that the continued behavior exhibited by the family group following years of aversive conditioning represented a threat to park visitors." The female grizzly was killed in August 2009 as the bears moved toward an occupied campground, and her yearling cubs were shot with tranquilizer darts with the intention of placing the two into captivity, but one died from the darting operation. The remaining cub was eventually placed in the Bronx Zoo.

The board of review concluded that the decision to remove the grizzly bear family group was appropriate under the park's bear management plan and guidelines.

Frank Miniter asserts, "Grizzly and black bear attacks on humans are at all-time highs in North America partly because bears are growing bold in areas where hunting is deemed politically incorrect."

Herrero wrote about this lack of hunting issue to a limited extent in his comprehensive book on bear attacks, *Bear Attacks: Their Causes and Avoidance*: "Hunting most species results in animals that avoid people, at least during the hunting season. Unhunted populations usually accept people at closer distances before fleeing. Hunting is one potential means of changing grizzly bear behavior so that surviving bears avoid people."

Others interested in the management of large predators take a different view. Former Banff park superintendent Kevin Van Tighem advocates that people need to stop being afraid of grizzly bears, and instead need to learn to live with them. He disagrees with the management philosophy of keeping bears afraid of humans and all that comes with that—hazing, aversive conditioning, the use of bear dogs, and relocating bears from conflict areas.

He told the *Calgary Herald*: "If we really want bears to have a future, we need to manage them without fear. The dominant management paradigm, certainly in Canada right through the 20th century, was that we could keep bears and people safe by keeping them scared of each other. We always have those messages, 'You are in bear country, all bears are potentially dangerous.' The whole idea was that if you avoid them, you will be OK."

He continued: "The day we have a calm mother grizzly bear hanging around Canmore—not getting into food and not harassing people—will be the day I know we have arrived." Van Tighem's view is counter to that offered by most bear managers and seems to have a low potential for becoming reality. The adoption of such a philosophy could result in more human injury and death since it fails to acknowledge that these are top-of-the-food-chain predators.

Paul Schullery, in *The Bears of Yellowstone*, wrote that bears in Yellowstone are safe from hunting, "but for generations the most aggressive ones, the ones most likely to attack humans or go after human food, have been the ones most likely to be removed from the population and given no opportunity to contribute to the gene pool." Schullery admits that the notion that hunting will make bears more wary of people is true, but is more complicated than most believe, involving a process of culling the most aggressive animals from the population.

Regulated harvesting through hunting is a management option bear managers are now preparing for in the Northern Rockies, but would, of course, be allowed only outside national parks. Park bear managers now put much of their focus on managing humans as they come into contact with grizzlies along national park roadsides.

As you walk in timbered areas, watch for bear signs, including claw marks on trees.

Avoiding
Grizzly Conflicts

As you hike or move around in the outdoors, generally try to be cautious, alert, and make noise. It's also recommended that your outdoor activities be conducted in daylight hours (avoiding dawn, dusk, and night), and in groups rather than alone. Yellowstone National Park officials report that 91 percent of the people injured by bears in the park since 1970 were hiking alone or were with only one other person. If children are in your group, keep them between adults, and review with them what to do in the event of a bear encounter. Never let children fall behind the group or run ahead to explore.

Make noise when you approach or are in brushy or woody areas where visibility is limited, or where rivers, streams, or other background noise could inhibit the sound of your approach. Areas of heavy cover and limited visibility are very dangerous for encounters between predators and humans. Talking loudly, singing, or whistling are good ways to let bears learn of your presence and move away, reducing the risk of a surprise encounter. Call out "hey bear, hey bear" as you proceed.

Try to be completely aware of your surroundings. Watch for bear signs, such as claw marks on trees, tracks or scat on the ground, upturned trees or rocks, and other vegetative disturbance indicating an animal has been digging.

If you smell an animal carcass, be sure to detour around that area since it would be a natural place to encounter a large predator. The presence of magpies or ravens also provides an indication that a carcass may be present. If you do find a fresh animal carcass, retreat from the area immediately, following the path from which you arrived.

Be aware that areas of berry abundance are also prime bear spots, as bears feed on berries in preparation for winter hibernation.

Do not wear headphones to listen to music while recreating (hiking, biking, jogging, etc.) in large-carnivore country. Pay attention, frequently looking around. If out with your canine friend, keep the dog on a leash. You do not want your unrestrained dog to go out exploring and return with a bear in its wake.

WARNING

BEAR

FREQUENTING AREA

Removal of this sign may result in INJURY to others
and is punishable by law

THERE IS NO GUARANTEE OF YOUR SAFETY
WHILE HIKING OR CAMPING IN BEAR COUNTRY

Bear frequenting area signs posted in national parks provide warning to visitors that there is no guarantee of safety in bear country.

Chapter 6

Greater Yellowstone Grizzlies

Erwin Evert was a happy man. A botanist, the seventy-year-old Evert had just finished publishing a 750-page book about plant life in the Yellowstone area, and he and his wife were enjoying their summer cabin, located in the Kitty Creek area just a few miles east of Yellowstone National Park. Evert took regular hikes into the nearby forest. In June 2010, a grizzly bear field research crew was working to capture and radio-collar grizzly bears in the area as part of the routine population-monitoring program for this federally protected species. Evert had a surprise encounter with an adult male bear that was recovering from sedation, and the encounter ended Evert's life.

That day—June 17, 2010—was a cold, windy day in western Wyoming, with sputtering snow showers. The two-man grizzly bear research team of Seth Thompson and Chad Dickinson had spent nearly a month setting traps for bears in the Kitty Creek area, but hadn't had much luck. This would be their last try, and with freshly set snares, the team headed up the trail on horseback. Thompson reported* that the team found an adult male grizzly in the first snare, and two other snares had been sprung, with no captures. The men darted the bear with a sedative and proceeded to process the bear, taking measurements and hair and blood samples, and placing a radio collar on the 430-pound, ten-year-old male. After completing their work, the men began packing up their gear and watched the bear begin to wake up and recover from the tranquilizer injection of Telazol. As the bear continued to recover, Thompson and Dickinson finished packing up, including pulling the signs that had been posted to warn the public that a bear-trapping effort was under way.

---

* Unless otherwise noted, all details of the grizzly bear attack on Erwin Evert are found in *Investigation Team Report—Fatality of Mr. Erwin Evert June 17, 2010*. U.S. Fish and Wildlife Service, July 16, 2010.

Thompson reported, "This was the final day of this trapping season and we knew we would not be returning for another trapping stint in the Kitty Creek drainage." They had not seen any hikers in the drainage for weeks and expected that the nasty weather conditions would curtail human activities in the area.

"We loaded the horses and mounted, and continued to watch the bear and stimulate it with noise," Thompson reported. "The bear was swaying its head laterally and tongue lolling, typical of a bear recovering from Telazol. After a while, we approached the bear from the relative safety of horseback. The bear could focus on us with its head up, and it was beginning to push up on its front legs. We were satisfied with the bear's recovery process and it was prudent for us to leave the site before the bear was fully ambulatory."

The team rode away and headed to check the last snare, which also held a grizzly bear, this one a four-year-old adult female that had been captured before. The men worked quickly, replacing the bear's radio collar with a new one, and retrieving the needed samples. The young bear began to recover from the tranquilizer as the men loaded their gear, again clapping and yelling at the bear to stimulate her, to assess her level of recovery. After removing all evidence of their presence, the men mounted their horses and waited. As the bear took to her feet, the men left the site and headed back down the trail that would lead them from the mountains.

Erwin Evert's wife, Yolanda, met Thompson and Dickinson near the Kitty Creek cabins. She asked if the team had seen her husband, who was late returning from his hike. They had not, but Dickinson agreed to try to find him, leaving Thompson near the road where he could call for help should Dickinson not return before dark.

Dickinson trotted his horse back to the site where the male grizzly had been captured and soon found Erwin Evert's body. A fatal bite to the head from a grizzly bear had ended his life. The grizzly was not in sight.

According to the investigative team report on this bear mauling, Evert knew that the bear researchers were trapping bears, and had expressed an interest in going to see what they were doing. He had reportedly been cautioned by a friend to stay away from such a dangerous situation.

The report noted, "There were no warning or closure signs at the incident location when Mr. Evert approached this site where he was killed." Evert had hiked about 1,700 feet off the main trail to the capture site, where he was attacked.

Bear managers ordered the newly collared male bear to be killed, and it was shot from a helicopter less than two miles from its original capture site. DNA tests later confirmed that this research bear had fatally mauled Evert.

Bears recovering from sedation are known to pose a threat to humans found nearby.

Since Evert's deadly encounter, the research team has modified its activities to include provisions for greater public notification of capture operations, including leaving the warning signs in place until three days after capture operations have ended. Yolanda Evert filed a wrongful death claim alleging negligence by

Bears that no longer avoid humans are deemed habituated.

the bear research team. A federal court judge in Wyoming denied the claim in 2012.

Research Bears

Bears recovering from sedation are known to be dangerous to humans; these bears are also in danger of attacks from other bears. Researchers documented one case in which a female grizzly bear recovering from sedation was charged and killed by an adult male grizzly. In another case, in September 1973, a wildlife manager was mauled and killed in Canada's Banff National Park when he moved too close to an adult male grizzly that was recovering from being tranquilized. In this case, the bear had a history of feeding on human foods and garbage and was being relocated via helicopter. A Parks Canada photographer had accompanied the bear biologist and their pilot to get footage for an educational film. While the bear came out of sedation, both the biologist and photographer approached the animal closely. The pilot left the two men filming on the ground and flew over the bear in his helicopter to see if it was still affected by the drug. The bear charged the helicopter several times, showing it had recovered from the drug. The pilot landed again, and the photographer and biologist continued to approach the bear, within about 100 feet. The bear charged, taking down the biologist and quickly biting him to death. The pilot chased the bear off the man's body with his helicopter and evacuated the unharmed photographer. They returned with armed guards within the hour, and the bear tried to attack the helicopter. The bear was shot and killed.

While bear handlers and researchers need to be sure a sedated animal is adequately recovering, they must also be aware of the danger as the bear does recover.

Habituation

Since 1973, grizzly bears in the lower forty-eight states have been protected under the federal Endangered Species Act. It is estimated the Yellowstone region contains at least 1,000 grizzly bears. Federal protection for grizzly bears has kept the animals free from human harvest or harassment, and has resulted in a population of large predators that have little reason to fear or avoid humans.

Bears that have lost their avoidance behavior toward humans are called "human habituated." Although most wild grizzlies will try to

Bears that approach human developments and receive food rewards will return to seek out food in a process called "food conditioning."

147

flee when first encountering a human, some bears seem to get used to people and do not run away if no negative experience is associated with those first human encounters.

Bears that become food conditioned are those that are attracted to human food or garbage because they were successful in accessing such food in the past. A bear that receives a food reward will seek out such food again because of the positive reinforcement of the reward.

Food-habituated bears become aggressive in their efforts to obtain food and must be destroyed.

As we have seen with a variety of predators, habituation may lead to attraction. But it's also important to note that there are human-habituated bears, and also those that seem to have a natural tolerance of human presence. Those that are naturally tolerant may not have ever had human contact in the past, while human-habituated bears have become so through repeated exposure to humans.

Bear managers view both human-habituated and food-habituated bears as presenting varied levels of danger to humans. Most food-habituated bears will eventually become aggressive in their efforts to access human food, and will damage property and injure humans in the process. For this reason, these bears are destroyed by grizzly bear managers.

Human-habituated grizzly bears are often seen along roads in national parks, especially in Yellowstone National Park, which receives more than three million human visitors each year. Grizzly bears foraging for natural foods and road-killed wildlife in Yellowstone will be seen by hundreds of human visitors as they drive by on the roadway. Many of these people stop to watch or photograph the bears they see, creating

Visitors to Grand Teton National Park line the roadway in a "bear jam," in response to the presence of a grizzly bear and her three two-year-old cubs in April 2013.

"bear jams," where traffic stops because of the presence of a bear. Once a bear learns there are no negative consequences from continuing to do what it is doing, it will become accustomed (habituated) to vehicle traffic and the presence of humans. Some bear experts do not believe such habituation is a bad thing, instead believing that habituated grizzly bears may be less prone to aggressively attacking humans during surprise encounters.

In the past, Yellowstone National Park officials tried to reduce the risk of conflicts between humans and grizzlies in the park by attempting to harass or haze the bears away from roadsides. Rangers would fire rubber bullets or loud cracker shells at the bears to scare them away. But bears are smart, and learned to recognize park vehicles and rangers, and even the distance the bullets could be fired. The bears avoided these circumstances, but would not flee from other people or cars. Aversive conditioning simply wasn't working, so Yellowstone officials changed the strategy from trying to manage the bears to managing the people who were encountering the bears.

Although Yellowstone officials have allowed grizzlies to become habituated to people, rangers now provide supervision and help to control human behavior during bear jams. Rangers hurry to the area where a grizzly has been spotted, and serve to control and educate the public about proper behavior around bears. Most importantly, rangers keep visitors from providing food rewards to the bears, which would create an extremely dangerous situation for both humans and the bears involved.

Visitors to Yellowstone National Park crowd in close to see and photograph grizzly bears. Many of these human-habituated bears have developed a tolerance for having humans at close range along roadsides.

One of the outcomes of having bears become habituated to humans in Yellowstone National Park is that humans have likewise become habituated to bears. Instead of keeping a distance from this potentially dangerous wild predator, people crowd in closer and closer, determined to get better photographs and see the animals up close. The public must continuously be reminded about the danger of such behavior.

Park service officials believe that tolerance of human-habituated grizzlies may allow for a higher density of bears in Yellowstone, since

Female grizzly bears with cubs pose special danger in human encounters, as the sows seem to make defensive attacks to protect their cubs.

bears can inhabit all parts of the park rather than avoiding areas near roadways and human developments. In addition, they believe that habituation may increase public appreciation and support for grizzly bears.

Yellowstone and other national parks with grizzly bears provide unique circumstances for both bears and humans, where there are strict controls on human behavior and development. Outside national parks, the situation is drastically different, and bear managers seek to keep grizzlies from becoming habituated to humans. Habituation in these areas may increase the likelihood of further human–grizzly bear encounters, and increase the risk that a grizzly will eventually maul or kill a human. Grizzly bear populations have recovered to the extent that the bears' range has grown far outside the boundaries of national parks. About half of the human–grizzly bear conflicts in the entire Yellowstone ecosystem (including national parks, national forests, state land, and private property in parts of three states) from 1992 through 2000 occurred on privately owned property.

Not All Grizzlies Are Created Equal

While all grizzly bears should be treated with caution, some grizzlies are naturally more aggressive than others. Many attacks on humans by grizzly bears involve female grizzlies with cubs, and in most cases appear to be females responding reflexively to an intrusion, called a defense reaction. Researchers also believe there is an overall decrease in aggression among females as their cubs get older.

Surprise encounters with grizzly bears in the backcountry account for a large number of human injuries reported, with 97 percent of hikers injured by bears reporting surprise as the reason for the encounter. Most of the injured hikers reacted to the encounter by running or attempting to climb trees, and 80 percent of those receiving severe injures from grizzlies had fought back or resisted rather than playing dead.

There are numerous reports each year of elk hunters who surprise a grizzly bear on a carcass, or return to a cached game animal to find a grizzly bear has claimed it—and the result is the bears maul the hunters.

Older grizzly bears are a special consideration as well, since evidence indicates that very old bears are particularly dangerous to humans. There have been numerous serious or fatal maulings by old grizzlies. In 1972, two campers were attacked in their Yellowstone campsite by a twenty-year-old grizzly, with one of the men killed and partially consumed by the bear after it had rummaged around in the campers' improperly stored groceries.

An old and aggressive bear in a national park in Alaska ended up breaking into numerous campers and garbage trucks before finally breaking into a ranger's cabin while the ranger was inside. And a young girl was killed and partially eaten by an old bear in 1967 in Montana's Glacier National Park.

In a 1976 paper at the Third International Conference on Bear Research and Management, Herrero concluded that for older bears, "It appears that difficulties in securing adequate food to maintain a healthy body weight may increase foraging motivation so that human food or garbage may be aggressively sought. The possibility that some old grizzly bears under special circumstances may be potential predators of man is also suggested by the data."

A month after Evert was killed by the drugged research bear in what appeared to be a surprise encounter, another series of grizzly bear attacks on humans took place outside Yellowstone National Park, but this is where the similarities end.

The Soda Butte Attacks

It was a dream trip for a forty-eight-year-old, stay-at-home dad raising his four children in Grand Rapids, Michigan. Kevin Kammer was on a fly-fishing adventure to the Rocky Mountains, camped just outside of Yellowstone National Park in the summer of 2010. He picked a campsite along Soda Butte Creek in a Gallatin National Forest campground, where he could hear the water loudly gurgling and running nearby as he lay in his tent. He knew he was in bear country because of all the signs posted, and he complied with the orders for proper food storage and keeping a clean camp.

He probably never heard the bear. He probably never heard the screams in the night coming from the two campsites upriver. Sometime around 2:30 a.m. on July 28, 2010, a bear attacked Kevin Kammer as he slept, pulling him from his tent along the noisy creek and killing him. By the time his body was found a few hours later, it had been partially consumed.*

---

* Unless otherwise noted, all details of the Soda Butte attacks are found in *Investigation Team Report—Bear Attacks in the Soda Butte Campground on July 28, 2010*. U.S. Fish and Wildlife Service, August 13, 2010.

Wildlife officials already knew that a bear had mauled two people in two separate campsites in the same campground during the night, and were working to wake everyone up and get them out since a dangerous bear was on the loose. It was during this process that Kevin Kammer's body was discovered, and wildlife agents learned it was now a man-killing bear. What they didn't know was whether it was a black bear or a grizzly bear, and they didn't know if the bear was alone.

National forests throughout the Greater Yellowstone ecosystem that are occupied by grizzly bears implement special rules for camping and food handling, as described in this highway sign near Cody, Wyoming.

The Soda Butte Campground was nearly full that night, with twenty-four of the twenty-seven available sites occupied by campers—some in hard-sided campers, others in tents. The first bear attack occurred at Campsite 16, where Ron Singer was sleeping in a tent with one other person and a small puppy. About 2 a.m., Singer was awakened by the sensation that the tent was moving, and he soon felt the pain of something biting his left leg through the side of the tent. Although he couldn't see the beast doing the damage, Singer, a former high school wrestler, began punching at the animal through the side of the tent, as his girlfriend screamed and hurried to turn on a light. The bear let go of Singer's leg and disappeared into the darkness. Singer never laid eyes on the animal that had attacked him. The occupants of a neighboring tent came to Singer's tent to apply first aid to his leg, and they soon heard a woman screaming from another campsite. Singer's group loaded him into a vehicle and left the area, driving to Cooke City, Montana, where there was cellular telephone service and emergency responders.

Just minutes after Singer was attacked, a second attack occurred at Campsite 11, where Deb Freele of Canada was sleeping alone in her tent. She awoke to the feel of the bear's teeth sinking into her upper left arm. The bear shook her briefly, and then let go of her upper arm, biting her lower arm. Freele screamed, but soon played dead, hoping the bear would leave. As the bear bit her on the leg before retreating, she could hear people yelling in the campground. She never saw the bear, which had mauled her through the side of her tent. Although she had bear spray with her in the tent, she never got to use it.

Other campers responded to Freele's cries for help, loading her into a vehicle and taking her to Cooke City, where they soon met up with the injured Singer and his party. Both Singer and Freele were taken to the hospital in Cody, Wyoming. Both would eventually recover from the injuries received in the maulings.

Emergency responders arriving at the campground included officials with Montana Fish, Wildlife & Parks, the US Forest Service, Yellowstone National Park, and the Park County Sheriff's Office. Teams of law enforcement officers drove through the campground, waking campers to notify them of the dangerous situation and evacuating the campground. It was during this process that Kevin Kammer's body was discovered.

Montana game warden captain Sam Sheppard received the phone call notifying him of a bear attack incident at 2:23 a.m., and he left his house fifteen minutes later, stopping to get a culvert bear trap on the way. Sheppard took authority of the incident command as soon as he entered the campground, and was soon joined by Montana game warden Jim Smolczynski. An initial security sweep did not reveal the presence of any bears, so Sheppard and Smolczynski began the process of investigating the scene at Kevin Kammer's campsite, and were joined by Montana bear specialist Kevin Frey. They knew that a bear was responsible, but beyond that, little was known.

The investigators found bear hair and bear paw prints on the tent. The paw prints included both big bear prints and small bear prints, but were somewhat unclear. Piles of scat were also discovered, and included both small scat and large scat. Frey concluded an adult bear and at least one smaller bear were involved, although the species could not be determined.

The investigators, using a team of armed officers as security as they searched through waist-high willows, expanded the search area to include what was soon discovered to be a well-used bear trail located between the campsite and Soda Butte Creek. Smolczynski collected more bear hair along this route and found more small bear tracks near the creek.

The investigators found several bear guard hairs that were light-tipped with underfur, consistent with known grizzly bear hair. More tracks were found in the sand along the creek, with claw marks indicating that a grizzly bear was the species involved.

The investigative team returned to the campsite, and a series of culvert traps were set in hopes of capturing the offending animal or animals. Kevin Kammer's tent was set up again in the location of the bear attack, and the largest bear trap was set just 6 feet away, with the rainfly from the tent draped across the trap, which was baited with meat. Two smaller culvert traps were placed nearby to capture smaller bears.

With the traps set, the investigators backtracked through the bear attacks of the night, arriving at Campsite 11, where Deb Freele had been mauled. Inside the tent, the team found a fragment of a broken bear tooth with a black cavity tract from the offending bear. A single bear hair was collected from inside Freele's shoe, which was found outside her tent. The team then proceeded to collect evidence from Campsite 16, where the first attack of the night had occurred.

Just a few hours after the traps had been set and the team moved away to keep the campsite free of human disturbance, an adult female grizzly bear entered the largest trap and was captured. The team waited a few hours in hopes any smaller bears could be trapped as well, but soon gave up and immobilized the adult bear with a sedative so she could be examined. Samples were taken of her blood, hair, and tissue. Sheppard inspected the grizzly's teeth and discovered that her upper right canine had recently been broken, and had a black cavity that appeared to match the broken tooth discovered in Freele's tent.

When young bears must be removed from the population after involvement in conflicts with humans, they are either euthanized or transported to captive facilities like zoos or education centers.

Although it appeared the offending bear had been captured, the job was far from over. The smaller bear or bears had to be captured, and the investigators needed conclusive proof that these were the offending animals. The samples were sent to a wildlife forensics lab in Wyoming for immediate examination, and the female bear was left in the trap. Sheppard spotted three yearling bears in the timber along the creek. The team once again backed off, leaving the traps to capture the young bears.

By the next morning, two of the three yearling grizzlies had been captured, but one remained outside, bluff-charging the traps several times. The remaining trap was reset and the team retreated to resume their wait. The next day, the remaining cub was captured, concluding the capture effort. A few hours later, the Wyoming wildlife forensics lab notified bear specialist Frey that DNA tests results provided a conclusive match between the captured adult female grizzly and the samples collected from the three attack sites. While the evidence did not indicate the yearling bears had been involved in the attacks on humans, the bears had participated in feeding on the third victim.

All four bears were transported out of the area, with the three cubs eventually transported to a zoo, where human visitors would view them without knowing they had fed on humans before arriving for their lives in captivity.

The adult female bear was taken to a Montana veterinary laboratory, where she was given a lethal drug injection. Once the bear was dead, a research team conducted a necropsy, an intensive evaluation of her body. Tissue samples were taken for further testing, as was the bear's brain so it could be tested for the deadly and dangerous disease rabies. The rabies test was imperative since there were two human victims who would have to be treated for rabies should the test come back positive. The test result was negative.

The single grizzly bear hair found on Freele's shoe did not match any of the four bears involved in this incident, indicating that there was a fifth bear at the campground. DNA analysis indicated that the fifth bear was the offspring of the adult female bear that had mauled the three people, perhaps born in a prior year. But there was no evidence this fifth bear was at any of the other attack sites. It is assumed that the fifth bear was a resident of the area, and that Freele had picked up the bear hair sometime during her two-week stay in the area.

What was the trigger that caused the adult female grizzly bear to prey on humans? The usual explanations involve the animal becoming habituated to humans, the bear receiving food rewards from humans, or the bear displaying surprise or defensive behavior in response to a human encounter. None applied in the Soda Butte case. In this case, the bear exhibited predatory behavior, specifically targeting humans as a food source. The investigation team report concluded that the attacks "cannot be clearly explained or understood."

The female weighed 216 pounds, which is thin, but within the range for adult female grizzlies with yearlings at that time of year. She had a moderate parasite load and was estimated to be between ten and fifteen years old.

The final investigative report noted these issues and added, "It is important to recognize that nutrition can be a contributing factor to stress in wildlife, but in and of itself, nutritional stress is not a sufficient explanation for predatory behavior by a bear on humans."

Researchers examined the hair, blood, and serum (a component of blood) from the adult female grizzly in an attempt to learn about her habits prior to the attacks. The levels of various isotopes (chemical elements) found in samples can be used to estimate the dietary history of an animal. Hair samples of different lengths can be used to learn if an animal's food habits changed over time, as revealed during the time the hair was growing. Grizzly bear hair grows at a rate of about 1.5 centimeters per month. Hair samples from the adult female grizzly involved in the attacks included a sample of faded, worn hair believed to have been shed the year before but still clinging to the current hair coat; a sample of new hair from the current growing year; and a mixture of the two. The hair samples were washed and ground, so the isotopes could be examined.

Stable isotope analysis indicated the female bear subsisted primarily on vegetation, with very little meat in her diet—with the result being a marginal level of quality nutrition to a bear already nutritionally stressed by the demands of raising three yearlings. Research indicates that 92 percent of grizzlies in the Yellowstone region consume a higher percentage of meat than this bear, which had relied almost exclusively on plants during the two years prior to the attacks.

Analysis of sulfur isotopes in bear hair, serum, and red blood cells can reveal whether animals are consuming whitebark pine seeds, which are often a preferred food source for grizzlies. Analysis of the sulfur isotopes for this bear indicated that she was not eating these seeds, even though they were abundant in the Soda Butte area.

Isotopes of carbon are used to examine whether an animal has consumed vegetation native to the Yellowstone region, which is associated with a C_3 metabolic pathway, or vegetation associated with a C_4 metabolic pathway, composed of a group of more tropical plants such as corn, sorghum, and sugarcane. The plants in the C_4 group are often associated with livestock feed and dog food, and livestock fed corn or corn-based feed show a C_4 signature in their meat. In addition, many human food products contain corn syrup, including granola bars, pop, and many baked and packaged foods. If a bear eats any of these foods (dog food, human food products, livestock, or livestock feed), researchers can detect the C_4 signature in the bear's carbon isotope. Research on the adult female bear involved in the July 2010 maulings indicated that the bear consumed little or no human-related foods, such as human garbage or pet food, during the two years prior to the attacks.

In all three maulings, the bear bit or ripped through the tent fabric or insect screen to reach the victims. One of the victims fought off the bear by punching it, while another made a noise and played dead. The first attack was on a person in a tent with another person and a dog, yet the other two attacks were on lone individuals. No food items or attractants were found in the victims' tents or campsites, and their fire pits were clean and free from garbage. Contents of the bear-proof food storage boxes did not include anything that would generate odors or aromatic attractants to bears. The bear was unmarked and had never been captured before, and had no prior history of conflicts with humans. There was no evidence the bear had ever consumed human-related foods or had been habituated to humans since she was rarely seen or reported.

"There is no clear explanation for the aggressive, predatory behavior of this adult female grizzly bear in the early morning hours of 28 July 2010," concluded the final investigation team report on the attacks.

More Fatalities

Fatal attacks on humans by grizzly bears in the Yellowstone region are becoming more common, and in 2011, there were two more human fatalities. One death occurred in July, and park officials noted the offending bear, a sow grizzly, had "acted in a purely defensive nature to protect her cubs. This female bear is not tagged or collared, and does not apparently have a history of aggression or human interaction." But a month later, the same adult female grizzly bear responsible for that death was linked to the death of a second man. Park officials then killed the 250-pound bear.

The investigative team report provides the chilling details of the first attack in 2011. At 11 a.m. on the morning of July 6, fifty-eight-year-old Brian Matayoshi and his wife, Marylyn, began a hike from the Wapiti Lake Trailhead in Yellowstone National Park's northern Hayden Valley. It's a very popular hiking trail in the Canyon area of the park, featuring open thermal areas interspersed with lodgepole pine timber stands. The trails are heavily used by hikers for day trips, as well as by those accessing the backcountry for longer excursions. Hayden Valley is world-renowned for its wildlife viewing, especially for the grizzly bear and bison that are commonly seen here.

One mile into their hike, the couple met another park visitor along the trail. They all stopped at a vantage point overlooking the valley and viewed a female grizzly bear and her two cubs from a distance of several hundred yards. The Matayoshis then proceeded down the trail and into the timber, but soon encountered a dense mosquito population that caused them to rethink their hike. The couple turned around and headed back down the trail they had just traversed, back toward the trailhead. By this time, the female grizzly had left the open meadow where she had been seen earlier and was now close to the trail. By the time the Matayoshis saw the bear, they were within 100 yards of her, so they turned around once again to move away from the large predator.

The sow grizzly saw the couple and gave chase. When the Matayoshis saw the bear begin to move in their direction, they began to run down the trail, yelling. The bear covered 173 yards quickly before hitting Brian, quickly mauling and killing him. Marylyn took cover behind a fallen tree just 5 yards from where Brian was being attacked. After killing Brian, the sow grizzly walked over to Marylyn, picked her up into the air by her backpack, and dropped her back onto the ground before leaving the scene. Marylyn was not physically injured in the attack and went to her husband's side. When she turned him over, the last breath of his life left his body.

The investigative team concluded that the incident "was initiated by a surprise encounter." Instead of fleeing, the grizzly sow chased down and attacked Brian Matayoshi, and the report noted: "What possibly began as an attempt by the bear to assess the Matayoshis' activities became a sustained pursuit of them as they fled running and yelling on the trail. In addition to the unfortunate circumstance of being at the wrong place at the wrong time, a possible contributing factor to the chase that ensued was that the victims ran from the bear while screaming and yelling." The sow grizzly that had killed Brian Matayoshi was not removed from the population or killed "due to the fact that the encounter was characteristic of a surprise encounter."

The decision not to kill the sow grizzly now known as the Wapiti sow was surely regretted later, when she was found to be involved in a second human mortality a month later.

WARNING

DUE TO BEAR DANGER AREA BEYOND THIS SIGN

CLOSED
TO ALL TRAVEL

Removal of this sign may result in INJURY to others and is punishable by law.

Date posted: 9/19/2011

A sign closing the Yellowstone National Park trail where a man was killed by a grizzly bear in 2011.

Fellow hikers discovered the remains of John Wallace, fifty-nine, of Michigan, on August 25, 2011, near the Mary Mountain Trail in northern Hayden Valley. His body had been partially consumed and was covered with debris, typical bear food-caching behavior. Wallace had hiked five miles up the trail, and what exactly happened there will never be known. What is known is that there were two bison carcasses in the area where Wallace's remains were found, and that there were sixteen bear bed sites around one of the carcasses located near the trail. Nine different grizzly bears, including a sow with two cubs, were seen there by another hiker just a few days before Wallace was killed.

After Wallace's body was recovered from the scene, investigators found fresh bear tracks in the dust of the trail where the body had been cached.* The tracks indicated an adult grizzly with two cubs had returned to the site where Wallace's body had been cached. Bloody cub paw prints indicated that an adult female grizzly with cubs "likely fed on or made contact with Mr. Wallace's body," the investigative team concluded. DNA testing on bear scat at the site confirmed that it originated with the sow grizzly involved in Matayoshi's death, which had taken place about a month earlier and 8 miles away. Other evidence at the scene indicated at least one other bear, a male of unknown age and species, had also made contact with Wallace, and that another adult female grizzly bear was also present at the site of the fatality.

Evidence indicates that Wallace had stopped on the trail for some reason at the time of the attack, and had faced a bear and tried to defend himself with his hands. There is no clear evidence indicating what prompted the bear or bears to attack Wallace, according to the investigative team's report, so it remains unknown whether the attack was defensive or predatory in nature.

The Wapiti sow was captured on September 28 and killed. Her cubs were live-captured and given to an institution to be raised in captivity. The reasons for the removal of all three bears were summarized as:

- The Wapiti sow and at least one of her cubs were present at the Wallace fatality site.
- The Wapiti sow may have been the bear that attacked and killed Wallace.
- Members of this grizzly family were very likely to have been involved in the consumption of Wallace's body.

The nature of the attack in the Wallace tragedy remains unknown. What is known about both the Matayoshi and Wallace fatalities is that neither of the hikers were carrying bear spray, their

---

* Information about the death of John Wallace is from the *Board of Review Report—Fatality of Mr. John L. Wallace from a Bear Attack on the Mary Mountain Trail in Yellowstone National Park*. National Park Service, August 25, 2011.

best possible defense in an attack. Yellowstone National Park averages about one bear attack on humans each year, but that number doubled in the tragic summer of 2011.

US Fish and Wildlife Service grizzly bear recovery coordinator Chris Servheen questioned whether the four fatal attacks on humans in the Yellowstone region in 2010 and 2011 were random events or evidence of something more. In a presentation delivered to a human–bear conflict workshop, Servheen noted: "There is no evidence to indicate that these were related to any particular factor. The only thing we do know is that human–bear encounter frequency is high because there are so many bears in the ecosystem."

Surprise Encounters

Shortly after dawn on Thanksgiving Day 2012, a forty-year-old man and his adult sons entered a timbered area along the Snake River in Grand Teton National Park, hoping to harvest an elk. The park's elk reduction program has been in place since 1950, and allows a limited number of elk to be harvested by special permit. Each hunter undergoes hunter safety and bear safety training prior to entering the field.

All three hunters had bear spray readily accessible, and the father was the first to notice the 500-pound adult male grizzly bear. Soon after it was noticed, the grizzly charged the group of hunters. The father began deploying his bear spray, while his sons both stood at the ready with their firearms. When the bear came within 10 feet of the young men, they both fired their rifles, with three bullets entering the bear and immediately dropping it to the ground. Investigators found a partially consumed and cached

The Jackson Hole and Greater Yellowstone Visitor Center, an interagency educational center located in Jackson Hole, Wyoming, has an extensive exhibit on grizzly bears, helping visitors entering the ecosystem become familiar with the species.

Yellowstone bear

elk carcass just 50 yards away, leading park biologists to conclude that the bear was defending its food source. The bear was estimated to have been nearly twenty years old.

Investigators concluded that the totality of circumstances "indicated that the hunters were forced to make rapid decisions in close proximity to the bear, and they acted in self-defense." No charges were filed against the men.

This was the first grizzly bear killed by hunters in Grand Teton National Park in the sixty-plus year history of the elk reduction program. The National Park Service noted: "To date, encounters between humans and grizzly bears that resulted in injuries to people are relatively uncommon. However, during the last twenty years as the Yellowstone ecosystem grizzly bear population has recovered and regained formerly occupied habitat (including in Grand Teton National Park), bear maulings have increased."

Grand Teton has documented six grizzly bear attacks on people since 1994, when a jogger was mauled on the Emma Matilda Lake Trail. Other maulings occurred in 2001, 2007, and 2011. None of these attacks resulted in fatal injuries to humans.

In April 2013, a forty-two-year-old student at Salish Kootenai College, on the Flathead Indian Reservation in northwestern Montana, was mauled by a grizzly sow near the college dormitory. Although injured, the student survived the attack. Tribal wildlife officials declined to take action against the animal, noting that the student had a surprise encounter with the sow and her two yearling cubs, and the sow reacted in a defensive manner.

That same month, an Alaska family had a terrifying encounter with a brown bear on the Kenai Peninsula. The family, a couple and their three children, had been bird watching and participating in a shorebird inventory when one of the children spotted a large sow brown bear approaching them. The family huddled together to appear larger and made noise to deter the bear, but the sow continued her approach. The father, forty-eight-year-old Toby Burke, stepped in front of his family and used a scope and tripod to push back against the attacking bear. The bear bit the scope off the tripod and struggled with Burke briefly before retreating. Burke received minor injuries in the wrestling match. Alaska state troopers arrived on the scene later and were tracking the bear's movements when it ran at the troopers, who shot and killed it. Officials also received reports of the bear's strange behavior, such as attacking a moving truck and a telephone pole and swatting at the river. The bear was a twenty-year-old female. Although she had recently emerged from hibernation, she was in good condition, with a layer of fat. Because of her erratic behavior, her remains were tested for rabies, but the results were negative. The necropsy did reveal that the bear was likely blind in one eye and partially blind in the other eye. It is unknown whether impaired vision was responsible for the bear's behavior.

Numerous grizzly bear attacks on humans were recorded in the Yellowstone region in the summer and fall of 2013. In June, a sixty-four-year-old rancher from Park County, Wyoming, was severely mauled by a grizzly while irrigating on his property outside of Cody. The man's dog first encountered the bear, which was a sow with cubs. Wildlife officials believe this was a defensive attack, with the man fighting back with his shovel. The man survived his injuries.

In August 2013, grizzly bears attacked two hikers and two researchers in two separate incidents on the same day. In one incident, two hikers had a surprise encounter with a grizzly bear cub on a trail in Yellowstone National Park. The sow suddenly appeared and charged the group, and the hikers deployed pepper spray and escaped from the area with minor injuries. The second incident that day occurred just outside the boundary of Yellowstone National Park, in eastern Idaho. A grizzly bear charged two researchers, knocking both men to the ground and inflicting numerous bites on one of the men. The bear quickly fled the scene, and officials marked this attack up to simply a surprise encounter.

Things were quiet for a month in the Yellowstone region, but in September 2013, a grizzly bear mauled a hunter in another surprise encounter in Wyoming's Teton Wilderness. The man broke his leg while trying to run from the bear and received bear bites during the attack as well. His injuries were not life threatening.

Future Hunts

In early 2013, the Interagency Grizzly Bear Committee (IGBC)—the consortium of state, federal, tribal, and Canadian resource management agencies charged with the recovery of grizzly bears in the United States south of Canada—endorsed the idea of eventually allowing regulated hunting of grizzly bears as populations recover. It was noted that rather than widespread harvests, the number of grizzlies to be harvested would be in the single digits. Hunting is already allowed in Canada and Alaska.

Idaho Fish and Game deputy director Jim Unsworth stated, "We have bears that are in conflict [with people], and certainly one of the ways that we could deal with that would be to reduce populations through hunting."

There was an outcry from bear advocates who protested the notion of eventually hunting bears, prompting the publication of an editorial coauthored by Harv Forsgren (regional forester for the US Forest Service and former chair of the IGBC) and Scott Talbott (Wyoming Game & Fish Department director and 2014 chair of the IGBC).

The men noted: "IGBC agencies have collectively and unanimously endorsed regulated hunting as one approach to promote coexistence, management of populations, and reduce conflicts between bears and humans."

The editorial continued: "As recovery efforts continue to succeed, bear populations will increase and bears will move into areas occupied by people and conflicts will increase. Unchecked grizzly populations in areas of high human density will compromise the value and tolerance people have for grizzlies. We know grizzly bears will require continuous management to ensure conflict with humans is minimized, and bear distribution and numbers align with social tolerances and biological suitable habitats."

Avoiding
Greater Yellowstone
Grizzly Conflicts

The US Fish and Wildlife Service recommends the following actions in close encounters with grizzly bears:

- If you surprise a bear at close range, drop a nonfood item (like a hat or bandanna) on the ground in front of you and slowly back away. Speak softly and avoid eye contact.
- Never run from a bear. Do not turn your back, but slowly and immediately leave the area if you can.
- If the bear charges, remain standing. The bear may be bluff charging, which is a warning for you to leave the area.
- Carry bear spray and spray the bear if it approaches too closely. If the grizzly bear does make physical contact with you after a surprise encounter, drop to the ground and play dead. Lie face down, leaving your backpack on. Cover your neck and head with your arms and hands, and curl up like a cannonball. Try not to move or make a noise. Once the bear moves off, remain where you are for as long as you can. Often a bear will move off a distance, but will return if it sees movement.

The National Park Service also recommends that if a grizzly bear approaches you in a persistent manner, with head up and ears erect, behaving in a curious or predatory manner, you need to be aggressive and fight back with fury if you hope to survive the encounter. Predatory bears do not give warning signals or use threat displays to attempt to scare you away, as a defensive bear will. A predatory bear will demonstrate its intense interest in you, often quietly, bearing in on you, eyes locked as it approaches. Predatory attacks end only when the bear is overpowered, scared away, injured, killed, or eats you.

Be aware of bear behavioral differences. If you believe that a bear is exhibiting predatory behavior, fight back as aggressively as you can. Use bear spray, rocks, knives, clubs, fists, loud noises, and firearms. Fight for your life!

If a bear attacks you at night in your tent, fight as hard and as loudly as you possibly can. Again, fight for your life!

The general rule of thumb for a grizzly bear attack is this: Play dead for a defensive attack, but fight against a predatory attack. The importance of knowing the difference between a predatory bear and a bear simply reacting to a surprise encounter cannot be overemphasized. Most of the time, a defensive bear will immediately initiate a charge, with head low, ears back, often veering away at the last second. In such surprise defensive encounters in Yellowstone National Park, bear–mauling victims who played dead received only minor injuries 75 percent of the time, while those who fought back received very severe injuries 80 percent of the time.

Human-habituated bears and food-habituated bears pose varied levels of risk to humans.

Chapter 7
Habituation and Alaska Attacks

Timothy Treadwell's adventures with bears were both unusual and ill-advised. The organization he helped to found, Grizzly People, called him the bear whisperer. According to the book he coauthored with Jewel Palovak (*Among Grizzlies: Living with Wild Bears in Alaska*), Treadwell had left his winter home in Malibu, California, to spend eight summers camped among the wild grizzlies of the Alaska coastline in Katmai National Park and Preserve. Katmai is one of the premier brown bear viewing areas in the world, with its population of more than 2,000 bears. There are several locations in that area where bears congregate to feast upon spawning salmon during a certain time of year.

Treadwell "immersed" himself among the grizzly population, lounging on the beach with bears as close as 15 feet, surrounding him on all sides. His thinking appeared to be that by emitting "unconditional love," the bears would come to accept him. When confronted with a population of more aggressive bears, Treadwell dressed in black from head to toe, rolled around in fresh bear beds to alter his human odor, and crawled around on all fours in front of the bears in an apparent effort to make his human body appear more bearlike.

One night, after reading a book about bear hunting, Treadwell found a sleeping bear outside his tent. According to the book, Treadwell, who talked to the bears a great deal, told this bear: "I'm ashamed to be human! I want to be like you, wild and free, liberated from the wicked ways of people."

In closing out the book, Treadwell claimed his greatest fear was that some people might attempt to copy his "past dangerous lifestyle" and be injured or killed in the process. He claimed to have changed his ways to a "much more conservative and respectful approach" when he returned to the area in 1996, backing off from his close observation of bears to a more remote way of studying them.

Treadwell did seem to want to become a bear, and in one of his last pieces of correspondence, less than a month before being killed by a 1,000-pound brown bear in 2003, Treadwell stated, "My transformation complete—a fully accepted wild animal—brother to these bears. I run free among them—with absolute love and respect for the animals."

Treadwell, forty-six, and his thirty-seven-year-old girlfriend, Amie Huguenard, camped with the Alaska brown bears again in 2003—Treadwell's thirteenth year of doing so. But this time, they stayed in the area later in the year. The frenzy of the migrating salmon was over—food was harder to find for the bears, and their behavior was more cranky and aggressive as the food source dwindled. Bears that had companionably feasted alongside each other just weeks prior began brawling, and the disputes involved increased aggression. Many bears began leaving the area, dispersing to find other food sources.

Treadwell watched and noted the increased danger posed by the bears, but still the couple stayed. The situation came to a head on October 5, 2003, when Treadwell and Huguenard were killed by a brown bear at their campsite. The attack that resulted in their deaths was not quick and merciful. It was brutal, tortuous, and long, documented in a six-minute audio recording of the event that was recovered by investigators after their deaths. It appeared the recorder's batteries went dead before Huguenard died, as her cries and wails reportedly continued as the recording ended. The tape was found in a camera near their bodies, which had been substantially eaten and buried with debris by the bear. The lens cap was still on the camera, so there were no images on the tape.

Craig Medred, outdoor editor for the *Anchorage Daily News*, covered the Treadwell story extensively, and much of this account of that night was pieced together from Medred's articles. It is believed that the attack began with Treadwell outside the tent at night. Treadwell called out to Huguenard, "Get out here. I'm getting killed." The recording indicated that Huguenard went out to help Treadwell and was then attacked and eventually killed by the same bear. When a pilot arrived for a scheduled pickup of the couple to take them from the area for the season, he discovered the disheveled campsite and a large bear standing atop a dirt mound near one of the tents.

When a team of investigators arrived on the scene in a float-plane later that day, the men shot and killed the large and aggressive bear that rose from its food cache of human remains and approached them. As the team worked to document the scene and recover what human remains they could, they could hear bears moving around in the brush nearby. Eventually they shot and killed a second bear that approached too closely as they worked. The team left the scene as darkness began to descend, and bad weather kept them from returning for a day. When the incident team returned to the Treadwell campsite, they inspected the body of the large male bear that had been guarding the cached bodies of the two people and found human remains and clothing in the bear's stomach. The bear was twenty-eight years old and weighed an estimated 1,000 pounds.

The board that investigated the two human deaths concluded that Treadwell had a long history of engaging in dangerous behavior while in the Katmai region, and that he had set up his campsite in a spot that would force bears to either wade in a lake or walk right next to the tent. Alaska Department of Fish and Game biologist Larry Van Daele was one of the investigators. He wrote that Treadwell's "behavior around bears, his choice of a campsite, and his decision not to have any defensive methods or bear deterrents in the camp, were responsible for this catastrophic event."

In that last piece of correspondence he'd written in the month before his death, Treadwell gave his view on the use of bear deterrents and defensive mechanisms: "People who knowingly enter bear habitat with pepper spray, guns, and electric fences are committing a crime to the animals. They begin with the accepted idea of bringing instruments of pain to the animals. If they are fearful, then they have no place in the land of this perfect animal."

Treadwell's philosophy led to the death of both himself and his girlfriend, and two of those bears that were so dear to him. If the couple had followed generally accepted safety precautions while in bear country, perhaps the attack and the resulting fatalities would not have happened. Instead, two human lives were lost, and two brown bears were killed as a result of the fatal attack.

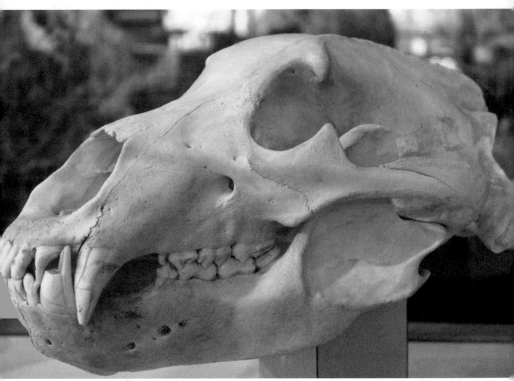

The skull of an adult male Alaskan brown bear is on display in the Grizzly & Wolf Discovery Center in West Yellowstone, Montana.

GRIZZLY, BROWN, OR KODIAK?

Alaska's brown bears, Kodiak bears, and grizzlies are all actually one species. Generally, Alaska "grizzlies" are those that live 100 miles or more inland, while coastal bears are called brown bears. Thanks to their rich diet of fish, coastal brown bears tend to be bigger than other grizzly populations. Kodiak brown bears are a different subspecies of grizzly bear that is geographically isolated on Kodiak Island in the Gulf of Alaska. Mature male bears in Katmai may weigh up to 900 pounds, while mature male grizzlies in Yellowstone may weigh up to about 700 pounds.

Alaska's brown bears, such as this one, are substantially larger than grizzlies in the Yellowstone region.

Rafter Assault

In July 2005, a Colorado couple was nearing the end of a ten-day rafting trip with their river guide in the Arctic National Wildlife Refuge when they spotted a brown bear near the riverbank. Hoping for an opportunity to observe and photograph this majestic symbol of wild Alaska, they paddled slowly. Soon it became obvious that something was not right. There were bits of camping gear scattered on the riverbank where the bear lingered, and a few scavenger birds sat nearby. As they moved to retreat, the bear began approaching the raft, eventually chasing the raft as it traversed the shallow river for nearly forty-five minutes, according to the story relayed in the *Los Angeles Times*. The river guide notified authorities, and the bear was shot at the site of the wrecked campsite, where it protected its food cache. Rick and Kathy Huffman, an Anchorage couple, had been killed in their tent by the 300-pound, nine-year-old bear. They had kept a clean camp during their rafting trip, and officials could find no explanation for what had provoked the attack.

Savage Student Encounters

The National Outdoor Leadership School (NOLS) was founded in 1965 by climbing guru Paul Petzoldt and is headquartered in Lander, Wyoming. NOLS bills itself as a global leader in wilderness education, taking students of all ages on backcountry expeditions to teach outdoor skills, leadership, and environmental ethics. In the summer of 2011, a backcountry expedition in Alaska resulted in four NOLS students being mauled by a single adult brown bear—one of the few such incidents of multiple victims in a single mauling, and the first such attack by a bear on a NOLS excursion.

According to the NOLS report on the attacks, on July 23, 2011, seven male teenagers were hiking in Alaska's Talkeetna Mountains, twenty-four days into a thirty-day NOLS course. This was the first day of a student-led expedition, in which students split into small groups for a three-day excursion without their instructors. The seven-member student group was two miles into its hike, and was traversing single file along a narrow creek, hiking in the shallow creekbed itself since it offered the path of least resistance through the tall brush. Practicing a bear-safety precaution, group members were calling out "hey ho" and "hey bear" as they hiked.

The student in the lead noticed a blonde-colored object off to his right as he passed by a rock outcrop. He turned to yell "bear" to the other students when he was attacked from behind, with the bear knocking him face-first into the water. His backpack remained on his back.

The next student in the line was 15 feet behind and saw the bear begin its attack. He turned and ran, but tripped and fell. He made it to the side of the creek, where he took off his pack and laid down in the bushes to hide. Three other students ran up the slope away from the creek, while two others started up the steep slope but one student turned back to the creekbed and was attacked by the bear. The bear quickly stopped its attack on the this boy, but when the student stood up, he was attacked again.

The student who had been hiding in the brush got up and was running toward the first victim when the bear attacked him. As the attacks continued, with some boys reporting being attacked more than once, a fourth student headed downstream, thinking he had escaped attack. He was wrong. The bear overcame him, and he fought back when attacked.

The well-worn teeth of a 17-year-old grizzly bear.

HOW EFFECTIVE IS BEAR SPRAY?

Tom Smith, Stephen Herrero, Terry DeBruyn and James Wilder coauthored a 2008 paper in the *Journal of Wildlife Management* titled "Efficacy of Bear Deterrent Spray in Alaska." The paper examined pepper spray incidents involving three species of bears in Alaska: brown bears, black bears, and polar bears.

People were able to use bear spray to halt attacks as follows:

- 92 percent of the time when used on brown bears
- 90 percent of the time when used on black bears
- 100 percent of the time when used on polar bears

The paper noted that of all persons carrying pepper sprays, 98 percent were uninjured by bears in close-range encounters.

The authors concluded, "Bear spray represents an effective alternative to lethal force and should be considered as an option for personal safety for those recreating and working in bear country."

Bear Outreach Education trailers are stationed throughout the western states during high-visitation periods to educate people about bear safety.

The NOLS investigative report noted that the students who had escaped the attacks by fleeing up the slope described the bear as "startled and confused—it would attack one person then look around and chase and attack someone else it saw." Although three of the students had bear spray, the spray was not used during the attack.

Grizzly bear conflicts can escalate during periods of food shortages.

The bear fled the scene, and the students came back together to initiate emergency medical procedures on the injured students, activating an emergency location beacon to notify officials that assistance was needed. It had begun to rain, so the students set up a tent nearby to wait for assistance. The uninjured students moved the injured students into the tent, and all seven students stayed inside for the five hours before an emergency helicopter arrived. The Alaska state trooper on the scene determined that two of the students needed evacuation by medical helicopter. All of the students were evacuated from the area by helicopters.

Three of the students were hospitalized, and all recovered from their injuries. The bear involved in this mauling incident was not seen again. Wildlife officials speculated that the bear was an adult sow with a cub nearby, and that the encounter was as much as a surprise to her as it was to her victims. It has also been suggested that the bear may have been defending a food cache.

More Fatalities

The bad news continued in Alaska, with two fatalities in two months in 2012. In August of that year, Denali National Park officials announced that three days into a backcountry hiking adventure, Richard White, forty-nine, of San Diego, California, was killed by a 600-pound male bear.

According to the National Park Service: "Three day hikers discovered an abandoned backpack and evidence of a violent struggle" along the river, and they immediately hiked back out to notify park service officials of the findings.

"Park rangers launched a helicopter and a fixed-wing aircraft from park headquarters that evening. At least one grizzly bear was still at the site, although there may have been multiple bears. The bear(s) moved away when the helicopter approached and landed. Two rangers on board the helicopter got out and confirmed the location of the victim's remains. After a short time a bear returned to the cache site while the rangers were investigating the scene, forcing the rangers to retreat to the gravel bar. The bear then began to circle around them. Rangers fired two rifle shots at the bear, but the bear was not hit. The rangers were able to leave by helicopter as darkness was setting in."

Alaska state troopers shot and killed the adult male brown bear that was defending the kill site along the Toklat River. The National Park Service termed the animal a "predatory bear."

Investigators found White's camera and reviewed the images it contained. The first photos of the bear were shot at a distance of 75 yards, and the bear had its head down in the vegetation. But the last photos showed the bear's head was up, as the animal was looking at, and moving toward, the photographer. It is not known whether the mauling occurred within seconds, minutes, or hours after White captured the images of the bear. Evidence on the scene indicated the attack occurred near the river's open, braided, gravel bar, and that the bear then dragged the remains to a more secluded, brushy cache site. Biologists estimated that about twelve grizzly bears had been residing in the vicinity of the kill site that summer.

A variety of wildlife and land managers work together as the Interagency Grizzly Bear Committee to educate the public about proper food storage in occupied grizzly bear habitat.

When a reporter affiliated with National Public Radio asked Denali park superintendent Paul Anderson whether it was the agency's policy to kill bears involved in attacks, Anderson responded in the affirmative, explaining that it is when a bear attacks a person and then identifies it as a food source. Anderson noted that in this case, the bear killed the person out on the gravel bar and then dragged him 150 yards into the brush where he partially buried him after having fed upon him for a period of time." Anderson continued, noting that the bear then "sat on that cache and wouldn't allow any other animals or humans to approach them without a fear of attack."

Anderson continued: "There have been documented incidents in the past, in other parks in the country, of bears that kill hikers or backpackers or people in the park and then feed upon them, continuing to do so. And we're not prepared to take that kind of risk here at Denali, given the proximity to hundreds of thousands of visitors."

Two months later, tragedy struck again in southeastern Alaska. This time, it was on Chichagof Island, 30 miles north of Sitka. The island is part of a chain of three including Admiralty, Baranof, and Chichagof—the "ABC Islands"—where one of the most dense populations of big brown bears are known to roam. The bears have a reputation for aggression, and research undertaken by a team led by James Cahill of the University of California, Santa Cruz (and published in the March 2013 issue of *PLOS Genetics*) has demonstrated that the ABC Islands brown bears show clear evidence of polar bear ancestry. Their research indicates this population derived from a population of polar bears likely stranded by receding ice at the end of the last glacial period. Since then, male brown bears migrated onto the islands, gradually evolving into a population that looks like brown bears, with polar bear genetics.

Passersby noticed an unsecured skiff on the beach, and when they stopped to see if assistance was needed, they were greeted by an aggressive sow bear and her cub. They retreated, but notified authorities of their find. Officials arrived at the site and found a campsite with evidence of a struggle. A trail of shredded clothing and trampled vegetation led investigators to where the bear had cached a man's partially consumed remains. The man killed by the bear was Tomas Puerta, fifty-four, of Sitka, who was returning to a forestry job site with a load of groceries when boat troubles apparently forced his stop at the beach. Wildlife officials killed at least one of the three bears found at the scene, but little is known about what prompted the attack on Puerta.

A month later, in November 2012, two trappers were mauled by a brown bear on the Kenai Peninsula. The men were setting snares in a wooded area along a river and couldn't see each other, but were within shouting distance. One of the men heard a roaring noise followed by his buddy's yells, so he ran to him and saw his companion being attacked by a brown bear. He yelled at the bear, at which point the bear turned the focus of its attack to him. The man played dead, so the bear returned to mauling its first victim. The bear eventually left and the men were able to get back on their boat and call for help. Both survived their injuries, although the first victim had severe injuries. It is not known what triggered the attack, but when one of the trappers returned to the site to retrieve the snares, he found bear cub tracks. Since the attack was in a remote location, authorities did not attempt to locate the bear involved.

There were numerous brown bear attacks in Alaska and Canada in 2013, most involving surprise encounters in areas of low visibility, defensive incidents involving sows with cubs, or bears defending carcasses. An exception occurred in an August 2013 attack in Alberta's William A. Switzer Provincial Park, when a grizzly bear attacked and bit a man sleeping in a tent with his wife. The couple escaped and called for help, while the bear tore through the tent and ransacked the campsite, where food was outside in coolers sitting atop a picnic table. The bear was shot and killed by wildlife officials, who had already tried aversive conditioning on the same bear earlier that day in a different location.

Making Sense of Bear Habituation

What conditions allowed Timothy Treadwell to so closely associate with grizzly bears in Alaska for thirteen years before being killed, when hikers in Yellowstone may be immediately attacked when encountering bears there? In 2005, Tom Smith, Stephen Herrero, and Terry DeBruyn published a comprehensive paper examining the overt-reaction distance of brown bears involved in aggressive-defensive attacks on humans. The paper, "Alaska Brown Bears, Humans, and Habituation," published in the scientific journal *Ursus*, indicated that the distance at which human presence triggers a charge is primarily a function of bear density (and its associated bear-to-bear habituation); and that greater distances are associated with lower bear densities.

The paper suggests:

1. The nutrient density of an area controls the number of bears it can support.

2. Bear-to-bear habituation is a product of bear density. Bears interact more frequently in areas with high bear densities, such as when bears congregate at a salmon-spawning area (thus promoting bear-to-bear habituation).

3. Bear-to-bear habituation may assist bear-to-human habituation. In these high-density bear areas, bears seem to have smaller "personal spaces" or overt-reaction distances. Thus, humans can be in closer association to bears than in lower-density populations, in which bears have a larger overt-reaction distance.

4. In some cases, humans lose their wariness of bears—this is human-to-bear habituation. This can be facilitated by the degree of bear-to-human habitation of an area. As the authors of the *Ursus* paper stated, "When people spend time around bears with very small overt-reaction distances, people tend to habituate to these bears, that is, they lose their wariness of bears."

The importance of seasonal food sources, such as spawning fish, is reflected in this bronze art that greets visitors entering the Grizzly & Wolf Discovery Center in West Yellowstone, Montana.

Aggregation of bears at feeding sites provides for great bear-viewing opportunities. Wildlife watching is an ever-growing pastime, and bear-viewing areas have been established at numerous locations, with Alaska's McNeil River Falls in the McNeil River State Game Refuge and State Game Sanctuary, and the Brooks River in Katmai National Park and Preserve growing in popularity. Brown bears are drawn to these areas in July and August as the chum salmon enter the streams to spawn and bears can feast. McNeil River is a state-managed unit that is tucked into the northern portion of Katmai National Park. The entire region is closed to the hunting of brown bears, although there are some hunting areas north of the game refuge, and within the Katmai National Preserve.

McNeil River Falls has been hosting humans to view brown bear aggregations since the 1940s. The activity became such a popular destination for photographers that state wildlife managers began regulating the number of visitors in the 1970s. The largest known gathering of brown bears in the world happens at McNeil River, and visitors apply for permits to visit, which are awarded through a lottery system. Each day, up to ten permit holders hike to one of the bear-viewing areas with an armed Alaska Department of Fish and Game naturalist. No one has ever been injured by a bear at McNeil River.

The Alaska Department of Fish and Game's management plan for the region notes: "The success of the visitor program at McNeil River is largely due to the habituation of bears to people. Habituation is defined as the reduction in the frequency or strength of response following repeated exposure to inconsequential stimulus. One type of response by bears toward people is aggression. Eliminating or diminishing this response creates a safer environment for interaction. Human actions that encourage habituation in bears also, by virtue of lowering stress levels in bears, encourages them to be comfortable around humans, which in turn enhances the viewing program."

The plan continues: "Most of the bears in the sanctuary are neutrally habituated. This means that while they are comfortable around people, they do not seek or receive human food or garbage."

The distinction between habituation and human food conditioning is an important one. Bears at places like McNeil River and Brooks River are habituated to the presence of humans, not to human foods.

Human food conditioning of bears requires two elements:

1. Bears have fed on human food or garbage.

2. Bears associate humans and/or human development as potential sources of food.

Larry Aumiller and Colleen Matt, wildlife managers at McNeil River for the Alaska Department of Fish and Game, noted that the agency sought to have brown bears become habituated to humans.

"We found that, in the absence of a food reward, habituated bears were safer than wary bears," stated Aumiller and Matt in a 1994 paper, "Management of McNeil River State Game Sanctuary for Viewing of Brown Bears."

Highly habituated bears at McNeil River perceive humans as neutral and not threatening. These habituated bears come closer to humans and exhibit fewer signs of stress.

Aumiller and Matt noted that not all bears at McNeil River exhibit the same level of habituation. Wary bears are not habituated to humans, and tend to flee from human encounters and avoid areas of human development. Neutrally habituated bears generally show indifference to humans, but to varied degrees. For example, some bears stay on the opposite riverbank from humans, while others tolerate humans at very close distances. Wildlife managers report that younger bears tend to habituate more quickly than older bears.

Habituation to humans at places like McNeil River is learned when bears must come near humans to access a food source (in this case, salmon). To get to the spawning salmon, bears have to overcome their wariness. Sow bears bring their cubs to McNeil River, providing learning experiences and habituation to humans at a young age. Sows in estrus that are already habituated to human presence will also draw more wary males with them to McNeil River, helping the habituation process along in bears that otherwise might not approach the area. Repeated neutral contact with humans reinforces the habituation process. The congregation of bears at McNeil River is an annual event involving many of the same bears—so much so that field guides are prepared to assist viewers in identifying individual bears that frequent the area.

At McNeil River, bears were habituated to neutral stimulus by consistent repetition. The same viewing areas and camp location are used without alteration. All humans use the same highly visible trails. Activities take place during the same hours each day. Human activity and behavior is tightly controlled during bear-viewing excursions, and there is an overriding emphasis on actions to prevent human food and garbage from being accessible to bears. Sanctuary staff observe individual bears closely and note their behavior, so that any undesirable behavior toward humans is corrected, with the goal of reinforcing habituation. Bears that approach too closely are warned away—sometimes quietly and sometimes in a more aggressive manner, depending upon the bear's behavior.

Things operate a little differently at the Brooks River bear-viewing area of Katmai National Park and Preserve. Three bear-viewing platforms are accessed by elevated boardwalks. The platforms have

Diversionary feeding of bears to reduce conflicts is the subject of much debate among wildlife managers.

a maximum carrying capacity of forty people, and on busy days, an on-site waiting list is used to accommodate viewing sessions lasting one hour each. Established trails and viewing structures are available for viewers, but visitors are permitted relatively unrestricted access throughout the area. Visitors are required to stay at least 50 meters from any single bear, and 100 meters from a sow with cubs. Campers must stay in the campground, which is enclosed by electric fences, or must camp a minimum of five miles beyond the area. Anglers must avoid the stretch of river near the fish ladder. Federal wildlife managers actively patrol the area, remain onsite, and engage in a variety of hazing practices to deter undesirable bear behavior.

Making human activities predictable helps to decrease risks of surprise encounters while encouraging habituation. But habituated bears approach people more often than nonhabituated bears, which can pose a danger to campers, according to Herrero.

"Once such a bear no longer avoids people the stage may be set for entering backcountry camps, especially if the bear has also learned to feed on people's foods," Herrero wrote in *Bear Attacks: Their Causes and Avoidance.*

BEAR HAZING

The Alaska Department of Fish and Game has issued a permit to authorized staff of the private, nonprofit Port Armstrong Hatchery to use electronic control devices (ECDs, manufactured by TASER International) to keep bears away from the salmon-hatchery facility located on Baranof Island in southeastern Alaska.

ECD testing at Port Armstrong began in 2010. "Bears were allowed to access the stream, but if they stepped into the work area, they were tasered and yelled at immediately." The device worked, with all the bears receiving a shot from the device leaving the scene. Some of the bears only retreated a distance, but none returned for more. And the biggest of the bears completely fled the scene.

The article quoted biologist Phil Mooney: "Mentally, I think it messes with the big bears much more." The article noted the ECD abruptly terminates the normal chain of posturing in a bear–human encounter and leaves the bear sprawling helpless on the ground. Of 110 brown bears shot by ECDs, 100 percent responded by fleeing the scene.

The ECDs are credited with preventing the loss of nine bears at the hatchery in 2012—bears that otherwise would likely have been shot in defense of life and property.

Smith, Herrero, and DeBruyn pointed out that, with the smaller overt-reaction distance at bear aggregation sites, "It is less likely a person will unintentionally trigger an aggressive response at aggregations."

They assert that "bear to bear habituation is primarily responsible for the tolerant demeanor bears often have toward one another, and this tolerance sets the stage for humans to commingle at close range without great risk." This is the best explanation as to why Treadwell's dangerous behavior was allowed to continue for so many years before his eventual demise. And it provides an indication as to why such behavior in an area like the backcountry of Yellowstone or Glacier National Parks would not be conducive to allowing people like Treadwell to survive close encounters with grizzlies.

Highway travelers leaving Dubois, Wyoming, and entering the Shoshone National Forest are warned to be bear aware.

Supplemental Feeding

Outside places with magnificent salmon-spawning runs like those described in Alaska, grizzlies are found at lower densities, with much larger overt-reaction distances. But the idea of increasing nutrients available to bears to draw them to feeding areas and away from people is an idea that is getting increased attention from bear managers across the large carnivore's range.

In the 1970s, Yellowstone grizzly researcher Frank C. Craighead Jr. noted that the earthen garbage dumps in Yellowstone had once served to zone grizzlies away from people during the busy summer tourist season, and suggested in his book, *Track of the Grizzly*, that managers should again consider "zoning grizzlies away from people by reestablishing one or more earth-filled dumps in isolated areas."

Craighead reported on his experimental use of baits to draw Yellowstone bears from the adjacent countryside, congregating them into a localized area. He reported that using elk carcasses to draw bears "was a proven and effective management tool for separating grizzlies and visitors, a function that had been performed by the dumps."

Many primitive campsites in national forests include warnings about attracting bears.

Alberta, Canada, wildlife officials already take part in an "intercept feeding program," in which road-killed wildlife are collected and stored during the winter months, then airlifted via helicopter to planned locations within spring grizzly bear range. According to the Parks Canada website, the idea is to "intercept" bears by keeping them away from livestock during the spring, until other natural food sources are available. Waterton Lakes National Park also allows "intercept" or "diversionary" feeding sites within park boundaries. Officials note that carrion is never placed near hiking trails, roads, or areas of human developments.

The International Association for Bear Research and Management (IBA) held a panel discussion on diversionary bear feeding that was summarized in its quarterly newsletter, *International Bear News*, in November 2011. Moderator Dave Garshelis of the Minnesota Department of Natural Resources noted some bear managers support diversionary feeding as a conflict-management tool.

Minnesota black bear expert Lynn Rogers advocates bear feeding in certain cases, noting that in one experiment, fed bears avoided people when not being fed, avoided campgrounds located near feeding sites, were involved in fewer conflicts, and were less likely to be killed than bears that were not fed, according to the *International Bear News* account. The IBA newsletter noted that shortly after the conference, "some bears from the Minnesota community where they are fed began getting into trouble, approaching occupied cars in a state park, breaking into a house, and even swatting a person who was attempting to approach a feeder in his yard. In the later case, the person (who received facial lacerations from the incident) tried to cover up the episode to protect the bears from potential agency retribution."

Other feeding programs offered a mixture of results. An illegal feeding program in the Lake Tahoe area of California and Nevada was undertaken during a severe drought in 2007, hoping to reduce the number of conflicts involving black bears breaking into homes. The program, carried out by a local bear advocacy group, was in violation of California state law prohibiting the feeding of wild animals, but did result in luring the bears away from homes, and the break-ins stopped, according to *International Bear News*.

Diversionary feeding near Aspen, Colorado, had less success. *International Bear News* reported that diversionary feeding "often cannot compete with original attractants, and sometimes increased local wildlife densities and conflicts." Managers continue to debate the merits and trade-offs associated with the short-term potential for reducing conflicts between bears and humans versus long-term dependency on feeding.

Future Management

Bear managers have achieved great success in reducing conflicts between grizzlies and humans, but as these populations continue to overlap across increased ranges, conflicts escalate. Some advocate habituation; others, avoidance.

Yellowstone National Park currently has sixteen special bear management areas in the park with high-density bear habitat, where restrictions on human use are imposed. Some of these areas are closed to human presence during certain seasons, while other restrictions include a minimum party size of four people, and limitations to travel in daylight hours only and to travel on established trails. The purpose of the closures are to prevent human–bear conflicts and provide areas where bears can pursue natural behavioral patterns and other activities free from human disturbance.

But roadsides in the park are a different matter.

Yellowstone National Park bear researcher Kerry Gunther reports that the park provides the perfect environment for bear habituation to people, with its relatively high numbers of bears and people, open habitat, relatively predictable human behavior, and low levels of human-caused bear mortalities. Although previous park service management had discouraged habituation through intensive efforts to manage bears (with adverse conditioning and removals), the emphasis is now on tolerating habituation and managing people at bear jams (rather than managing bears). This change in management philosophy has had results on the ground. Traffic congestion caused by bear viewing is increasing in both number of cars and duration, and bears are approaching closer to the roadsides during such encounters. Bear managers like Gunther now wonder how close bears and humans can interact under such circumstances without injury. Others ponder the difference between these roadside interactions and backcountry encounters, and the levels of risk of human injury associated with both.

Chris Servheen, grizzly bear recovery coordinator for the US Fish and Wildlife Service, points to emerging issues with grizzlies and humans. Servheen reports that as grizzly populations have expanded outside national parks, bears are now utilizing open agricultural areas like grain and alfalfa fields, and showing a lack of avoidance behavior toward humans. In addition, residents in rural and agricultural areas that followed suggested guidelines for eliminating or securing bear attractants now find that bears have moved into their neighborhoods anyway, and reside there for a portion of the year. This is causing significant increases in conflicts. According to Servheen, no one factor is responsible—the increase is due to a combination of more bears across a wider range, more human development, and fluctuations in natural food sources.

ELECTRIC FENCES

Many recreationists in bear country now use portable electric fences or pens around their campsites to deter bears from attempting to enter the sites. Portable electric pens are also used to protect domestic sheep herds at night in grizzly range in Wyoming's Bridger-Teton National Forest.

Former United States Geological Survey research ecologist Tom S. Smith of the Alaska Science Center (now at Brigham Young University in Utah) recommends electric fences be used for long-term field camps; for hunting camps where game meat and trophies are stored; in areas with high bear numbers; and in areas problem bears are known to frequent. The electric fences not only protect people and gear, but teach bears a good lesson about avoiding camps.

At the time of this writing, electric fences are not approved by federal officials in the lower forty-eight states in areas where food-storage orders are in place.

Chapter 8

Learning to Coexist with Predators

Increases in both human and predator populations come with an increased risk of attacks on humans in areas where these populations overlap. A great variety in the circumstances leads to predator attacks on humans, from surprise encounters in which the predator reacts defensively (such as a sow bear protecting her cubs) to those involving predators that stalk and kill humans as prey (as mountain lions have done in numerous cases). Michael R. Conover, editor of the scientific journal *Human–Wildlife Interactions*, has noted that neither human nor predator is responsible for predator attacks, "and nothing is gained by trying to identify which party is the culprit." To a certain extent, this is true.

A person involved in a group outing on a sunny afternoon on a popular hiking trail may have no warning that a black bear in the area considers humans a prey species. But we know that certain actions decrease the likelihood of predator attacks on humans. Keeping a clean camp, free of items that could attract wild animals, has become common practice when camping in "bear country," as is harassing coyotes away from school playgrounds. What appears to be uncommon, however, is the knowledge that what was once remote "predator country" now encompasses many residential neighborhoods across the countryside.

Many of the predator attacks on humans described in this book occurred in areas where there are severe restrictions on hunting, or where the animals are granted nearly complete protection from persecution. In these cases, the predators have either lost their fear of humans or otherwise became habituated to human presence. These animals have no *reason* to fear and avoid man, and in some cases are rewarded by contact with their human neighbors.

Wild predators that receive food rewards from humans quickly become dangerous, exhibiting increasing levels of aggression toward humans, as has been documented numerous times with coyotes and grizzly bears. Unfortunately, some people seem to believe that predators are inhabitants of remote wilderness areas and the far woods, and not present in their neighborhoods. They may leave dog food and garbage outside, or feed deer in their yards—endangering themselves, their neighbors, and wild animals.

Others attempt to excuse the majority of predator attacks on humans as cases involving illness, starvation, or loss of natural foods, but this is rarely the case. While it is true that humans have moved into wild lands, forcing predators into closer association, the larger view is that human developments and landscape improvements provide enriched habitats for prey species and the predators that key on them. If rabbits and rodents enjoy the enhanced habitats and move into them, small predators like coyotes are sure to follow. Elk and deer move into residential areas to browse on ornamental shrubs, lawns, and trees planted by homeowners—and sometimes these animals move into residential areas to lessen their risk of attack by predators like wolves. When met with little discouragement, eventually the larger predators follow.

A century ago, the human response to predators approaching at close range was predictable. The animals were shot on sight, and surviving predators were thus wary, keeping their distance and fleeing at the sight of a human. Decades of persecution and unregulated killing of predators led to severe population declines. Changing public attitudes eventually led to restrictions on harming endangered animals like gray wolves and grizzly bears. Regulated hunting seasons were established for other predators, such as mountain lions and black bears. Recovery of predator populations has been successful across the country.

Conservation measures have been so successful that, as Conover noted in his 2008 *Human–Wildlife Conflicts* paper, "Why Are So Many People Attacked by Predators?", "Many predators have now learned that humans make good neighbors." We are such good neighbors, in fact, that we now have five North American predator species that attack, injure, and kill humans: wolves, coyotes, mountain lions, black bears, and grizzly bears.

Humans have encouraged (both intentionally and unintentionally) the presence of wild predators in their neighborhoods. As human developments are created and expand, land managers often plan for open or "green" spaces, recognizing that our quality of life is enhanced by the presence of natural areas and wildlife. It is a thrill to see a wild animal at close range and to feel a connection with nature. But the downside to our increased tolerance for wild animals near humans is often discounted. We tend to disregard the notion that close association with a wild animal can lead to tragedy for both human and animal. Predators can, and do, kill people. From the lowly coyote to the charismatic grizzly bear, wild predators inflict harm on people when their association is too close. It does a disservice to both human and animal to ignore or deny this reality.

In many cases involving human habituation of predators, patterns of behavior indicated the risk of attack was increasing. That pattern consisted of increasing reports of predator observations in residential areas, especially during the daylight hours, followed by attacks on pets, and eventually the aggression included attacks on humans, some of which were fatal. This pattern is evident in numerous mountain lion conflicts, as well as in conflicts with coyotes: First the animal is detected, then seen in residential yards during the day, then pets start disappearing, then a human is attacked or threatened, and finally the offending animal is killed. A similar pattern was demonstrated in the 2013 black bear attack on the Florida woman recounted earlier.

There is some variation in the proper way to respond to an attacking predator, but a general rule is that, if it is anything other than a grizzly bear, fight aggressively for your life. If you have a surprise encounter with a grizzly bear and it attacks, playing dead has been effective at lessening or stopping the attack. But any predator that attacks you as you sleep in a tent should be fought as aggressively as possible. In nearly all cases involving predators, unless an escape to safety (such as a secure building) is very close, running away is not an option.

There is debate among wildlife professionals as to whether firearms are an effective defense in attacks by grizzly bears. The US Fish and Wildlife Service maintains that, overall, bear spray is the best method for fending off an attacking grizzly. Federal law enforcement agents found that people who encountered grizzly bears and used a firearm in self-defense suffered injuries about 50 percent of the time. During the same period, those who defended themselves with pepper spray escaped injury most of the time. Those who did suffer attacks had less severe injuries. There is less debate about the effectiveness of using a firearm to defend against other predator species. Even a small-caliber firearm can kill or disable a coyote, wolf, or mountain lion, or deter an attacking black bear.

A last lesson from the predator attacks examined in this book lies in the human responsibility to manage predators in a way that protects human health and safety. Wildlife managers must be given the flexibility to respond to changing conditions within predator populations, including the ability to condition predator populations in a way that trains the animals to avoid humans. This usually involves a combination of aversive conditioning techniques on problem animals and public hunting of wild animal populations. But in some areas (such as in national parks or municipal areas), it may require agency action via lethal control. Predator populations can survive and thrive despite lethal control of individual members of the population. Failure to take action can be predicted to lead to predators preying on humans.

Management Changes, Predator by Predator

How you deal with the management of one predator can vary widely from how you manage another. For example, the National Park Service change in management from hazing bears away from people along the roadside in Yellowstone National Park to instead managing people at bear jams appears to be reflected in how Yellowstone officials are managing wolf watchers in the park, and that raises concerns for wolf managers.

Human-habituated predators like wolves in national parks can range far in their travels, coming into close contact with humans outside the security of park boundaries.

"From a management perspective, that is a disaster," said Mike Jimenez of the US Fish and Wildlife Service in an interview. "That doesn't contribute to keeping animals wild. It doesn't contribute to having animals learn where it's appropriate or inappropriate to be around people, and that's a very tough thing to balance out."

Why should anyone outside the park be worried? Because wolves, like bears, are far-ranging predators that will not spend their entire lives in park boundaries, but will carry life experiences from the park forever. The wolf-watching sessions in Yellowstone appear to be at a greater distance than most of the bear-watching sessions, but there is concern that, as people and wolves continue to be comfortable around each other, that distance will narrow.

Wolves that then leave the park and have encounters with humans will not have a ranger present to provide educational narratives, and wolves will encounter a potential prey base consisting of livestock and pets, with no reason to have any negative view of the danger of approaching humans.

"It's a real problem," Jimenez said, and one that wildlife managers will continue to struggle with in the future.

Most black bear attacks on humans are predatory in nature and inflicted by adult male bears during daylight hours. A bear exhibiting predatory behavior toward a human is usually silent as it intently stalks its human prey, or pulls a person from a tent in the darkness of night. In either of these cases—bold daylight or nighttime predatory attacks—fighting vigorously for your life is your only option. Wildlife managers recognize that the danger to other humans will not decrease until the offending bear is killed.

Wolf attacks on humans occur during daylight hours and with little or no warning to the intended victims (although some encounters that did not escalate to attacks seemed to involve prey-testing behavior by the wolves). In most known cases of wolves inflicting injuries on humans, the wolves demonstrated increasingly fearless behavior. Indeed, the common thread in all North American wolf attacks involving human injury seems to be a loss of fear of humans. Wolf habituation to human presence occurs as the result of nonconsequential encounters, but the transition from nonaggressive behavior to aggressive attack can be rapid and unpredictable. A wolf approaching human development without fear, or approaching humans, is a recipe for disaster. Federal wolf manager Mike Jimenez stated it frankly: "Predators near people, near housing, is a bad idea."

Generally, if you encounter a wolf or wolves that are vocalizing at you, they may be defending a den or rendezvous site, so deliberate retreat is your recommended action. But a wolf or wolves moving toward you, perhaps seemingly in a playful manner, should be treated to a show of aggression.

Most coyote attacks occur during the day, and usually are preceded by bold behavior clearly indicative that the animals have lost their fear of man (such as coyotes killing pets in yards, frequent daylight encounters with humans, etc.). In many cases, problem coyotes have received food rewards from previous human encounters and, similar to their wolf counterparts, will also engage in prey-testing behavior. To reduce the risk of coyote attacks, humans must be proactive in coyote encounters, discouraging the animals from a close association with human settlements. Hazing bold or aggressive coyotes rarely works; lethal removal of the offending animals is the only effective strategy to ensure human safety.

Mountain lion attacks on humans are usually preceded by an increase in mountain lion sightings in residential areas, attacks on pets, and other behavior indicating the animals are no longer wary of human presence. Most mountain lion attacks on humans are predatory in nature, and humans should fight back aggressively to save their lives. Again, wildlife managers must take action to ensure human safety when these large predators turn toward humans as possible prey.

What Actions Are Appropriate?

With recent attacks by large predators (both lethal and nonlethal), natural resource and wildlife management agencies are no doubt reexamining their roles in providing for human safety—an issue that is subject to debate, as is what control measures are appropriate in each circumstance. Animal advocates in some communities propose that only nonlethal control measures be deployed, but wildlife managers concerned with human safety prefer immediate lethal action to resolve conflicts. Translocation of dangerous predators into other areas only places the risk in a different area—it does not lessen the danger.

In accordance with the experts quoted in this book, I recommend the following actions to reduce the risk of predator attacks on humans:

- Reduce predator attractants in residential areas, and keep clean camps when in the backcountry.
- Be aware of factors that indicate the risk of attack is increasing, such as predators being seen repeatedly in daylight hours, or dangerous situations such as reports of garbage-raiding bears or coyotes that have been fed in neighborhoods.

- Change the behavior of predators to reinforce a fear of humans. This may include hunting predators, aversive conditioning, or removal of individual animals by wildlife managers.

- Alter human behavior so that people keep their distance from wild animals, in recognition that predators kill to survive and that humans have varied (and often undetermined) levels of risk of becoming prey.

Author Jim Sterba noted in his 2012 book, *Nature Wars*: "The idea of wildlife overabundance is difficult for many people to accept. We have been trying to nurture wild populations back to health and protect them from human despoliation for so long that it is hard to believe we have too many of them or that people might need protection from them."

Public attitudes about predator management continue to evolve—from early overexploitation to the conservation-oriented approach that led to recovery programs. The five North American predator species discussed in this book have reached or exceeded biologic recovery goals, with a positive change in the numbers of the animals present on the landscape across a broader range. A consequence of this success is an increased human tolerance for the presence of predators and, subsequently, an increased risk of attacks on humans by predators that have long lost a reason to be wary of their human neighbors. Having high predator populations near urban areas is a known factor in increased risk of attacks on humans.

There remains a commonsense tendency to review safety precautions when it comes to outdoor recreation or backcountry expeditions. But what about people who reside full-time within the range of these predator species? Most view a suggestion that a person should not walk out their door or down a sidewalk in their community without bear spray attached to their belt as unreasonable. To ensure human safety, focus must not just be on backcountry encounters, but should center on reshaping our current predator–human relationship to one of mutual wariness and respect, with the recognition that the relationship can just as easily become that of predator and prey.

It is time for another shift in public thinking, to acknowledge that our efforts must now turn to keeping our distance from the animals, for the good of both human and animal populations. Focus should be on not just reconditioning predator populations to be wary of humans, but on altering human behavior in the same way for humans to once again become wary of wild predators, animals that by definition kill to survive.

Management of wild predators includes a responsibility to manage predators in a way that protects human health and safety, while conditioning predator populations to avoid humans.

Source Notes and Recommended Reading

From the Introduction

Kertson, Brian N., R. D. Spencer, and Christian E. Grue. "Demographic Influences on Cougar Residential Use and Interactions with People in Western Washington." *Journal of Mammalogy* 94(2), 2013: 269–281.

Löe, Jonny, and Eivin Röskaft. "Large Carnivores and Human Safety: A Review," *AMBIO: A Journal of the Human Environment* 33 (6), 2004: 283–288.

Merkle, Jerod A., H. S. Robinson, P. R. Krausman, and Paul Alaback. "Food Availability and Foraging Near Human Developments by Black Bears," *Journal of Mammalogy* 94(2), 2013: 378–385.

From the Black Bears chapter

Gunther, K. A., and H. E. Hoekstra. "Bear-Inflicted Human Injuries in Yellowstone National Park, 1970–1994." *Ursus* 10, 1998: 377–384.

Herrero, Stephen, A. Higgins, J. E. Cardoza, L. I. Hajduk, and T. S. Smith. "Fatal Attacks by American Black Bear on People: 1900–2009." *Journal of Wildlife Management* 75(3), 2011: 596–603.

Kaniut, Larry. *Alaska Bear Tales*. Portland, OR: Alaska Northwest Books, 2003.

Madison, Joseph S. "Yosemite National Park: The Continuous Evolution of Human–Black Bear Conflict Management." *Human–Wildlife Conflicts* 2(2), 2008: 160–167.

From the Coyotes chapter

Foster, D. R., G. Motzkin, D. Bernardos, and J. Cardoza. "Wildlife Dynamics in the Changing New England Landscape." *Journal of Biogeography* 29, 2002: 1337–1357. Doi:10.1046/j.1365-2699.2002.00759.x.

Schmidt, R. H., and R. M. Timm. "Bad Dogs: Why Do Coyotes and Other Canids Become Unruly?" in *Proceedings of the 21st Vertebrate Pest Conference*. Davis: University of California, Davis, 2007: 287–302.

Timm, Robert M., R. O. Baker, J. R. Bennett, and C. C. Coolahan. "Coyote Attacks: An Increasing Suburban Problem," in *Proceedings of the 21st Vertebrate Pest Conference*. Davis: University of California, Davis, 2004: 47–57.

Timm, Robert M., and Rex O. Baker. "A History of Urban Coyote Problems." Wildlife Damage Management Conferences, Internet Center for Wildlife Damage Management. Lincoln: University of Nebraska, 2007.

White, L. A., and S. D. Gehrt. "Coyote Attacks on Humans in the United States and Canada." *Human Dimensions of Wildlife* 14, 2009: 419–432.

Whittaker, D., and R. L. Knight. "Understanding Wildlife Responses to Humans." *Wildlife Society Bulletin* 26, 1998: 312–317.

From the Gray Wolves chapter

Butler, L., B. Dale, K. Beckmen, and S. Farley. 2011. *Findings Related to the March 2010 Fatal Wolf Attack near Chignik Lake, Alaska.* Wildlife Special Publication, ADF&G/DWC/WSP-2011-2. Palmer, Alaska.

Fritts, S. H., R. O. Stephenson, R. D. Hayes, and L. Boitani. "Wolves and Humans," in *Wolves: Behavior, Ecology, and Conservation* (L. D. Mech and L. Boitani, eds.). Chicago: University of Chicago Press, 2003: 289–316.

Geist, Valerius. "Death by Wolves and the Power of Myths: The Kenton Carnegie Tragedy." *Fair Chase* 33, 2008.

Linnell, J. D. C., R. Andersen, Z. Andersone, L. Balciauskas, J. C. Blanco, L. Boitani, S. Brainerd, U. Beitenmoser, I. Kojola, O. Liberg, J. Loe, H. Okarma, H. C. Pedersen, C. Promberger, H. Sand, E. J. Solberg, H. Valdmann, and P. Wabakken. "The Fear of Wolves: A Review of Wolf Attacks on Humans." *NINA Oppdragsmelding* 731, 2002: 1–65.

"Management of Habituated Wolves in Yellowstone National Park." Yellowstone National Park, 2003.

McNay, Mark E. "A Case History of Wolf–Human Encounters in Alaska and Canada," in *Wildlife Technical Bulletin* 13. Juneau: Alaska Department of Fish and Game, 2002.

McNay, Mark E., and Philip W. Mooney. "Attempted Predation of a Child by a Gray Wolf, Canis Lupus, near Icy Bay, Alaska." *The Canadian Field–Naturalist* 119(2), 2005: 197–201.

From the Mountain Lions chapter

Baron, David. *The Beast in the Garden.* New York: W. W. Norton and Company, 2004.

Beier, Paul. 1991. "Cougar Attacks on Humans in the United States and Canada." *Wildlife Society Bulletin* 19, 1991: 403–412.

Benson, D. E. "Bridging Philosophy and Management for Lions and People," in *Proceedings of Mountain Lion–Human Interaction Symposium* (C. S. Braun, ed.), 1991: 83–85.

California Department of Fish and Game. "Trends in Mountain Lion Encounters." dfg.ca.gov/news/issues/lion/trends.html. 2009. Accessed July 20, 2011.

Deurbrouck, Jo. *Stalked by a Mountain Lion: Fear, Fact, and the Uncertain Future of Cougars in America.* Guilford, CT: FalconGuides, 2007.

Etling, Kathy. *Cougar Attacks: Encounters of the Worst Kind.* Guilford, CT: Lyons Press, 2004.

Fitzhugh, E. Lee. "Managing with Potential for Lion Attacks Against Humans," in *Proceedings of the 3rd Mountain Lion Workshop* (R. H. Smith, ed.), 1988: 74–77.

Fitzhugh, E. L., and D. P. Fjelline. "Puma Behaviors during Encounters with Humans and Appropriate Human Responses," in *Proceedings of the 5th Mountain Lion Workshop* (W. D. Padley, ed.), 1997: 26–28.

Fitzhugh, E. L., S. Schmid-Holmes, M. W. Kenyon, and K. Etling. "Lessening the Impact of a Puma Attack on a Human," in *Proceedings of the 7th Mountain Lion Workshop* (S. A. Becker, D. D. Bjornlie, F. G. Lindzey, and D. S. Moody, eds.), 2003: 89–103.

Gross, Liza. "No Place for Predators?" Public Library of Science, 2008.

Hebert, D., and D. Lay. "Cougar–Human Interactions in British Columbia," in *Proceedings of the 5th Mountain Lion Workshop* (W. D. Padley, ed.), 1997: 44–45.

Howard, Walter E. "Why Lions Need to Be Hunted," in *Proceedings of the 3rd Mountain Lion Workshop* (R. H. Smith, ed.), 1988: 66–68.

Mattson, D., K. Logan, and L. Sweanor. "Factors Governing Risk of Cougar Attacks on Humans." *Human–Wildlife Interactions* 5(1), 2011: 135–158.

From the Grizzly Bear chapters
Cahill, J. A., R. E. Green, T. L. Fulton, M. Stiller, F. Jay, et al. "Genomic Evidence for Island Population Conversion Resolves Conflicting Theories of Polar Bear Evolution." *PLOS Genetics* 9(3), 2013: e1003345. Doi:10.1371/journal.pgen.1003345.

Craighead, Frank C. *Track of the Grizzly.* San Francisco: Sierra Club Books, 1979.

Gunther, K. A., M. A. Haroldson, K. Frye, S. L. Cain, J. Copeland, and C. C. Schwartz. "Grizzly Bear–Human Conflicts in the Greater Yellowstone Ecosystem, 1992–2000." *Ursus,* 14(1), 2004: 10–22.

Gunther, K. A. and H. E. Hoekstra. "Bear-Inflicted Human Injuries in Yellowstone National Park, 1970–1994." *Ursus* 10, 1998: 377–384.

Gunther, K. A., and T. Wyman. "Human Habituated Bears: The Next Challenge in Bear Management in Yellowstone National Park." *Yellowstone Science* 16(2), 2008: 35–41.

Herrero, S. M. "Conflicts between Man and Grizzly Bears in the National Parks of North America," in *Bears: Their Biology and Management*, vol. 3. From a selection of papers from the Third International Conference on Bear Research and Management. International Union for the Conservation of Nature Publications, New Series No. 40, 1976: 121–145.

Herrero, Stephen. *Bear Attacks: Their Causes and Avoidance*. Guilford, CT: Lyons Press, 2012.

Miniter, Frank. *The Politically Incorrect Guide to Hunting*. Washington, DC: Regnery Publishing, 2007.

Olsen, Jack. *Night of the Grizzlies*. New York: G. P. Putnam's Sons, 1969.

Schullery, Paul. *The Bears of Yellowstone*. Tucson, AZ: Harbinger House, 1992.

Smith, T. S., S. Herrero, and T. D. DeBruyn. "Alaska Brown Bears, Humans, and Habituation." *Ursus* 16, 2005: 1–10.

Smith, T. S., S. Herrero, and J. M. Wilder. "Efficacy of Bear Deterrent Spray in Alaska." *Journal of Wildlife Management* 72(3), 2008: 640–645.

From the Learning to Coexist with Predators chapter

Aumiller, L. D., and C. A. Matt. "Management of McNeil River State Game Sanctuary for Viewing of Brown Bears." International Conference on Bear Research and Management 9, 1994: 51–61.

Conover, Michael R. "Why Are So Many People Attacked by Predators?" *Human–Wildlife Interactions* 47, 2008. http://digitalcommons.unl.edu/hwi/47.

Sterba, Jim. *Nature Wars: The Incredible Story of How Wildlife Comebacks Turned Backyards into Battlegrounds*. New York: Crown, 2012.

Index

About the Author

Cat Urbigkit is an award-winning writer and photographer. She has written ten books, including *Yellowstone Wolves: A Chronicle of the Animal, the People, and the Politics* and *Shepherds of Coyote Rocks: Public Lands, Private Herds, and the Natural World*. She maintains the WolfWatch newsblog and contributes regularly to regional newspapers and other outdoor blogs. She lives in western Wyoming.